# Happily Divorced

# Happily Divorced

A Journey Through Divorce
& Co-Parenting by the Golden Rule

## Teresa Harlow
### with Bob and Ian Harlow

Copyright © 2019 Teresa L. Harlow
Lewis Center, Ohio 43035
All rights reserved.

ISBN-13: 978-0-578-49830-0

Editing: Karen Heise
Cover Illustration: Madison Luse
About the Author Photography: Kiki Israel

Library of Congress Control Number:2019910801
First Edition 2019

For Ian

We did it all for you!

Love,

Mom (and Dad)

## *Table of Contents*

Foreword by Bob Harlow......................................................................xi

Introduction ........................................................................................ 1

    A Son's Perspective................................................................ 7

Chapter 1 In the Beginning: Splitting Our Assets................................. 9

Chapter 2 Shared Parenting: It's Not a Competition ......................... 15

Chapter 3 School Days: Parents & Teachers Take Note .................. 21

    A Son's Perspective.............................................................. 23

Chapter 4 Living in Two Homes: A Family Guide ............................. 25

Chapter 5 Motorcycles, Boats, & Conflicts: Oh My! .......................... 31

Chapter 6 Reconciliation: Nice But No Dice ..................................... 41

Chapter 7 In Laws: If You Like Them, Keep Them! .......................... 49

    My Mother-in-Law................................................................. 50

    My Sister-in-Law................................................................... 51

    A Child Among Us ............................................................... 52

    Miss Independent? ............................................................... 52

    Divorcing the Extended Family ............................................ 53

Putting it All Back Together .................................................. 54

A Son's Perspective............................................................ 55

Chapter 8 The Friendship Web: A Tangled Mess for Divorcees ........ 57

Chapter 9 Single Life: Weird Conversations with the Ex .................. 63

Chapter 10 Rebounders: A Cautionary Tale...................................... 67

Chapter 11 Meeting the Ex's New Someone: Do I Have to? ............. 71

Chapter 12 Shaky Ground: Bringing New Adults into Our Child's Life 75

The Introduction................................................................... 78

Chapter 13 Happy Holidays: Are They Still Possible?........................ 81

Halloween .......................................................... 83

Thanksgiving ........................................................ 85

Christmas............................................................. 86

Chapter 14 Birthdays: Shared Celebrations ...................................... 89

Chapter 15 Soccer Mom (and Dad): Don't Miss Out! ........................ 93

Chapter 16 Co-Pawrenting: It's Your Child's Dog .............................. 97

Chapter 17 Vacations: Overcoming a Scheduling Nightmare...........101

Chapter 18 Nurturing a Child's Talents: Our Budding Musician........107

Chapter 19 Discipline: A United Front..............................................119

A Son's Perspective..........................................................125

Chapter 20 Helping Each Other: Divorced Parents Do This Too ......127

Chapter 21 Finances After Divorce: Still a Joint Venture...................131

Chapter 22 Graduation Part 1: High School Comes to an End.........143

Chapter 23 The Harlows: The Real Modern Family .......................... 149

Chapter 24 Graduation Part 2: Our Boy is a College Grad ............... 153

Chapter 25 Stepparenting: What New Fresh Hell is This? ............... 163

    Of course we're all evil! ...................................................... 163

    Parenting Styles ................................................................ 164

    Blending Parenting Styles ................................................. 165

    Brandi ................................................................................ 166

    Have I left anything out? .................................................... 169

Chapter 26 In the (New) Beginning: Our Son is All Grown Up .......... 171

Afterword: Revisiting My Mission ..................................................... 175

Acknowledgements .......................................................................... 179

About the Author .............................................................................. 185

## *Foreword by Bob Harlow*

My phone rings. I look down, and the Caller ID says "Teresa Harlow," the ex-wife. Now that our son has graduated college and moved out of town, we don't talk as often as we used to, but it's always nice to hear from her. So I answer the phone, exchange pleasantries, and ask, "What's up?"

She tells me she has an idea for a book she is just starting to write, and she has a few things to run by me. "Writing a book?" I ask. "What's it about?" "Well," she answers, "it's about us." "About us? In what way? Is it fiction? A murder mystery?" (LOL)

"No," she answers. "It's about us and our relationship after the divorce as co-parents of Ian. It's called *Happily Divorced,* and I was hoping you might be interested in possibly being a part of it. I'm going to write about our divorce and how we decided to put our differences aside and raise our son together in the best possible way that we could as a divorced family." "Sounds interesting," I respond. "But how can I be a part of your book?"

"I'm thinking after each chapter or so that I write you could come up with a couple of paragraphs from your perspective to include. What do you think?" I answer that I'm intrigued and ask her to give me some more details; we talk for another 30 minutes, and I agree to be a part of her book. I hang up the phone and think, "Man, she might be onto something here. What could possibly go wrong?"

So a few weeks later, I get the first chapter, and after reading it I come up with a paragraph or two of charming, witty comments to add. A couple weeks later, I get the next chapter, and again I come up with a paragraph or two of charming, witty, hilarious comments. Then the 3rd chapter arrives, and it's about the actual end to our marriage in the early stages. So I'm reading this chapter. . . this story of our life. . . and as I'm reading it, I notice this version is much different than the version I've told countless times over the years. So I go back and read it again, and as I'm reading it, I get a little more upset with each passing sentence.

At this point, I decide to give her a call, and I get her voicemail. I leave her a message about my concerns and ask for a return call when she has a minute. So a few days pass with no phone call, but I do receive the next chapter from her, which I immediately read and find myself even madder than after the chapter before. I reply to her email that I'm not happy. She suggests I take a break from reading the next couple of chapters, blogs, or posts until she has some time to consider my concerns and get back to me.

So here we are almost 20 years after our divorce, 20 years of rebuilding our friendship. And now the book about this very effort could ruin everything. This could have ended our relationship . . . the friendship that we worked so hard to maintain. There were some pretty heated emails flung back and forth between us coupled with Facebook "unfriending" and some time off from each other. But we didn't resort to what many divorced couples do when they get mad at each other. There were no public attacks with horrible and hateful words through social media or even through mutual friends and family. We didn't do or say anything that we possibly couldn't come back from. We went to our neutral corners for a while. Even though we were mad at each other, we still respected each other for the amazing job we did raising our son.

Turns out, we used the same formula to come through this conflict as we had used for the entirety of our divorced relationship. We put our mutual respect for each other as parents of our son first.

A couple months into our time-out from one another, my stepdad passes away . . . my son's grandpa or "Pops" as Ian had always called him. As we always did, we put our differences aside for the best of the family. Ian and I welcomed Teresa at the viewing and funeral and the family gathering after the funeral. We were respectful to each other as we always had been even when we were angry at one another. We always did the right thing when we needed to, and we never went to that place to which there was no return.

About 8 months go by, and nothing had really changed between us – we were still not really talking, and I'd made an effort not to read any new chapters that were posted online. Then one day, I get a phone call. The Caller ID again says, "Teresa Harlow." The ex-wife.

I cautiously answer the phone. "Hello, what's up?" She responds that she's been doing some serious thinking. She read the book beginning to end trying as best she could to put herself in my shoes. As a result, she decided to revise the book pretty substantially and asks if I might be willing to take another shot at reading it. Not sure if this is a good or bad idea for me personally, I decide to go along for now. "Sure, why not?" Turns out she had actually printed a copy for me and asked me if she can bring it to me in person so we could talk a bit. I agree that it sounded like a good idea, and we scheduled a day and time to meet.

Teresa showed up to the house, manuscript in hand, and we sat down and talked a bit. She hands me the pages of her new and improved *Happily Divorced* book – the version you are about to read.

*Teresa Harlow*

She invited me to highlight anything in the book that still bothered me so that we could discuss it. I told her I probably wouldn't get around to reading it until the next weekend. But as it turned out, I really wanted to see if it read and felt different to me this time. So I began reading it that evening. About 9 chapters in, I hadn't found the need to highlight a thing, and I texted her to let her know we were on a much better path this time. It wasn't that all the painful stuff had been removed. But it sure felt more balanced. And I didn't feel like I was being cast as the villain in the story.

I'm not going to tell you if you read this book that your divorce is going to be perfect. That's impossible. Divorce is a failure of something that was supposed to last a lifetime. But it also doesn't mean you have to hate your ex or present the worst version of yourself to him or her for the rest of your life. If you read this book and you try to do what we did, who knows? You might find yourself writing the Foreword to your ex-wife's first book. You may actually look back proudly on how you handled what normally is a death sentence for the majority of divorced couples' friendships.

Reading these pages and looking back on the past 20 years, I have to say I'm proud of our marriage, divorce, and the rebuilding of our friendship. Hell, I'm even proud of how we handled the first draft of this book. Even though we didn't agree, we found a way through mutual respect to do the right thing. If divorce is the path you're on or have already gone down, and you are getting ready to read this I book, I hope it will help you, too (or you two) to become *Happily Divorced*.

## *Introduction*

I want to invite you on a journey – a journey through our life of divorce with a child. Oh God, that sounds awful! Who would want to be dragged through that? Who? Oh, wait – I see the problem. I forgot a word in the preceding statement. It was meant to read "a journey through our *happy* life of divorce with a child." A little better, right?

―――――――――――――――

It was July 5, 1999. Just typing the date still brings tears to my eyes as I remember the overwhelming feeling of despair when I realized my so-called "nuclear family" would not survive. It's funny that I write those words given the fact I really don't know what they mean. I think it has something to do with the traditional family unit we picture from the 1950s and '60s: father, mother, brother, sister, dog, and cat . . . or something like that. When a major element of the family falls away, particularly a parent, there is no longer a predefined expectation of happily ever after. Again, what the hell is *that*?

Even after twenty years, I sit here with tears streaming down my face as I again re-live the possibility that in that moment when I chose to tell my then-spouse that I wanted a divorce, we could have lost it all. But we didn't. And I think it is because we both held and still hold such high hopes and love for our family that we were simply unwilling to let it die. No, it didn't die. But it did, in fact, take on a new and most interesting form that the world rarely witnesses. We went from being the husband, wife, and son to being the father, the mother, and son quite seamlessly. Are you sitting there asking yourself why I think this is such a big deal and why you might spend your precious time reading such a seemingly uninteresting tale?

As it turns out, what we accomplished with far less effort than we were expending trying to hold our little family unit together is something that makes sense – a construct that allows us all to thrive and follow the life paths we are each meant to lead—lives that include not only respect for one another but also true friendship and real love. That's right. In divorce, my ex-spouse and I found a way to maintain our love, albeit of a new flavor, and our family. And I don't mean we got through it or we avoided confrontation or we just minimized interactions. We actually found a more conducive model within which our family could thrive and be truly happy. Crazy talk, right?

I know. It sounds impossible. And if I hadn't been a co-producer of these results, I, too, would probably think, "This woman is nuts and must be exaggerating. Her ex and her son must see it differently." Well, in case you doubt the experience which I am about to share with you, I have included the perspectives of my son and his father who participated in our unique approach to "happily ever after."

Why am I sharing our story? To begin, I'm very proud of the life we've created. When I sit and think about it, I actually revel in our accomplishment. In fact, achieving this saved my soul, which otherwise might have disintegrated into a million pieces and blown away. Second, I see way too many unhappily divorced families. And for that matter, I know of way too many married couples who stay together "for the sake of the kids." I'm convinced they're doing the kids (and themselves) more harm than good. So I want to paint a picture of a model of family life many may not have considered an option. Maybe you're newly divorced and not sure if it is even possible to save your family. Maybe you feel you would have a better shot at happiness if you divorced, but you can't face the possible death of the family. I'm here to tell you that you don't have to. But there are a few prerequisites to consider.

First, I highly doubt that the *Happily Divorced* family model will work where violent behavior of any sort exists between family members. I'm not talking about the uncharacteristic outbursts that take place at the onset of the divorce scenario, but rather, real violent behavior displayed by either spouse. Second, it is unlikely this will work if you really don't share the same core moral values of the other person. Sure, you can be mad at the other person, whether because you are hurt, they cheated on you, or they always put you down. These may only be symptoms of an unworkable living arrangement. But at the end of the day, you should be able to consider this person someone with whom you share a common definition of what is right and wrong. If you are unsure whether you can fulfill this last prerequisite, I would say you probably can unless you *know* you can't. If your spouse stole from you or killed your pet or beat you, this probably won't work for you. Otherwise, it may be worth giving this a shot.

I know. We are hard-wired to think we must dislike our exes. We couldn't possibly respect them, or God forbid even *like* them and still call ourselves "good" exes. Could we? Wouldn't that be a clear violation of the *ex-spouse code*? To like and care about a former partner after all attempts at reconciliation have been abandoned? Aren't you just supposed to write them off at that point, declare your losses, admit you chose badly, and work to minimize the damage to the rest of your life –

especially the damage thrust on your kids? Oh, the *kids.* That is for sure the worst part of it.

STOP IT! It doesn't have to be all negative. You don't have to hate your spouse. In fact, I'm going to grant you a license right now to continue to admire, respect, and maybe even like him or her – if you so choose.

Now, I'm not saying every ex-spouse is worthy of our admiration, respect, or anything else. Some are really horrible. Physical abusers and deadbeats should all be put in jail as far as I'm concerned.

But for those of us who simply find our life paths, dreams, desires, and personalities have parted ways, your relationship can actually be much, much better as a divorced "couple" than it ever could have been if you would have chosen to forcibly stay together against your inner will.

Before you think about writing me a tersely written email, please realize that I'm not suggesting you cut and run at the first, second or even hundredth argument you have with your spouse. Quite the contrary! After all, you did take a vow for better or worse. So you owe it to each other and to your child or children to work as hard as you can to overcome those *worse* moments and remain an intact family. Pull out all the stops. Talk it through, move or change jobs, seek therapy, whatever! I'm not going to lie. Some of the situations we encountered as divorced parents were simply less than ideal. And to avoid it destroying our family required tremendous effort and choosing very carefully.

Shortly before Bob and I separated, a friend of mine shared with me that he and his spouse were divorcing. I offered my condolences. He told me not to be sorry. They had just decided that they could not be happy together anymore. He said, "I don't hate her. And why should I have to? I chose to be with her in the first place because there were things about her that I love. That doesn't become untrue because we are divorcing." I thought, "*Wow, what a mature perspective.*" Until that moment, I hadn't realized that way of thinking was even an option.

After my marriage ended, I spent 4 years in a relationship with another man for whom I deeply cared. But just as if I had finished reading a book, the story ended along with our relationship. At first, this man started down a path of vengeful ugly behavior meant to degrade me. At that time, I reminded him that while things may not be good any longer, we have many wonderful snapshots to carry around in our hearts of those happy times. And I asked him not to destroy those photos, those memories. The good times. They still happened. Even when we parted.

Just like that, the ugly behavior and accusations ceased. In fact, after a year or so, this man and I were able to coexist among our tightly intertwined friend group with relative ease and complete civility toward one another. And yes, I still do carry those snapshots of our good times around in my heart.

What I share with you here in this book is not a guide or a how-to. And it is absolutely not intended to pass judgment on those who don't handle their situations the way we did. It is just an account of the many ways in which our lives and relationships have evolved since that fateful day in 1999. I have changed the names of friends and others beyond the immediate family out of courtesy and respect for their privacy. Still, I feel compelled to share our story since so many have told us how great it is that we have created this unique approach to post-divorce family happiness.

The other possible outcome of reading this book is you might discover there is more to think about when contemplating divorce than simply seeking to "fall in love" again. For instance, have you thought about your parenting and living arrangements? How about your shared friendships and your in-laws? Do you have any recollection at all of what it is like to be single (which may sound great right now, but actually sucks if you ask me)? For many of you, there will be rebound relationships and maybe even attempted reconciliations with the ex. Have you contemplated all the stuff your kid does that you both want to be there for? And I haven't even gotten to legal matters, schooling, planning vacations, discipline, finances, new relationships, birthdays, and other celebrations. There is *a lot* to consider!

You may simply look at this list and be struck by the number of situations you will inevitably have to navigate differently as a divorced couple than as a married couple. It may prompt you to think long and hard on the idea and consider going to greater lengths to preserve your family unit in the more conventional sense. Trust me. All of this wasn't easy, and I look with envy on many of my friends who seem to have figured it out, stayed together, and still live under the same roof.

Whatever you decide, I hope you'll choose happiness because I'm here to tell you it is absolutely an option! Now . . . here's to family,

*Bob, Ian, and Teresa Harlow*

friendship, and love always.

## *A Son's Perspective*

I remember the day my parents told me they were getting a divorce. They were both sitting on the couch next to each other, crying, not necessarily holding each other. Through tears and deep, broken breaths, they explained to me what was going to happen. I don't know how much I actually understood at the time, but I do remember walking outside by myself after my parents had finished detailing the situation. I was pointing at the ground, cursing the devil, saying it was his fault that my parents were getting a divorce. As I look back on that now, watching five-year-old me standing in the back yard blaming Lucifer for my parents' separation, I definitely chuckle – for many reasons.

I was under the impression that everything in my life was about to change dramatically and for the worst. While things did change A LOT, I cannot remember a time when my life was specifically bad as a result of my parents' divorce. I never felt the need to choose between one parent or the other; I never felt a competition between my parents for my affection; I never feared my family was going to disappear.

It can be hard to really analyze a situation when you are engulfed in it. Sometimes, an outside perspective or different point of view can really shed light on the unknown. Watching other friends' experiences with their nuclear families hitting full meltdown gave me this outside perspective. I watched their families turn from love to hate in a matter of months. I watched my friends struggle with the pressure of feeling like they had to choose one parent over the other knowing full well that whichever parent wasn't chosen would be heartbroken if not actually angry. That sounds like the most unfair, stressful thing to put anyone through, especially a child. I'm not sure how my parents did it, but they avoided all of these horrible situations that seem so stereotypical in divorced families. I always felt equal love from both of my parents and still do to this day, and I share the exact same, in return.

## *Chapter 1*
## *In the Beginning: Splitting Our Assets*

Our co-parenting journey wasn't all rosy from the beginning. There were ugly words, failed reconciliation attempts, and at least one call to the sheriff during our tumultuous early days of separation. I feared I would lose my son, my home, and the rest of what was important to me at any given moment. In addition to having to face the loss of my spouse, albeit my decision, I was also facing the loss of his family with whom I was very close. While my family all lived more than a thousand miles away, his was local. His mom treated me like a daughter, and I was even the matron-of-honor in his sister's wedding just a month before our separation. So, in the beginning, they all hated me. And I could see why. He was their son and brother. They saw me as the person who was ripping the family apart. And I felt that burden deeply.

But that is not to say that the separation and the divorce were entirely my fault, either. I'm not writing this to fall on a sword here in some veiled attempt at redemption. No. While I may have been the one who called it, it usually takes two to screw things up in a marriage. For years, I had warned that we were headed for divorce. But those warnings did not result in resolution of the underlying problems on either side. So there was plenty of blame to go around. I just ended up being the one who insisted on that final, fateful move to a different life.

My son's father, Bob warned me that if we divorced I'd be missing out on half of my son's life. The gravity of those words still haunts me. And the reality of it now still brings tears to my eyes. But feeling the time I would spend with them was going to be miserable for everyone, the quality of our lives had to come first.

For me, it was the notion that I might miss out on half of my son's life that motivated me to find a better way forward for all of us. I didn't want to lose that much. I didn't want my son's father to lose that much either. I didn't hate him. I just didn't want to live with him. And I certainly didn't want my son to suffer that much loss.

So I focused on our friendship and those things about Bob that I like. He had always been a great father and good friend. He's quite a comedian, too. And I was going to miss that probably the most in my daily life, that and the fact that he did most of the cleaning around the house. Yeah, I know you're probably wondering why I so desperately had to get out of this relationship. But as that is not the focus of this book, or anything that should have went any differently given where our lives have led us now, I will just say I had reasons I felt were justified, right or wrong. It doesn't matter now, and everyone's happy. And I have no doubt that as I write this book, my reasoning behind this decision will surface.

So we set about the messy business of separating while working together to minimize the impact on our five-year-old son, whom we both loved more than life itself.

First, there was the immediate need to relieve the tension that comes from cohabitating with someone from whom you are divorcing. The negative energy is overwhelming, and at times, all-out debilitating.

## Happily Divorced

It's like watching someone die – that someone was our marriage, our dream family. Very depressing. But as neither of us could afford to just take time off from work to sort through all this, we had to come up with another interim solution. We ended up splitting weeks in the house. One week I would stay there with our son and Bob would stay with family. The next week Bob would stay in the house with our son and I would go to my girlfriend's house and stay in her guest room. We talked about what to do with our home, and ultimately, we concluded that neither of us could afford it alone as we were a two-income household by necessity. So we sold it and divided the proceeds. Selling it was hard since we had only built the place two years earlier and Bob had just spent a lot of time finishing much of the basement. I loved that house. But in the end, it was better to leave the negative energy we had deposited there behind as we started our new lives.

We talked about how we would divide other things up, too, right down to the CD collection. Fortunately, neither of us got super-territorial over the small stuff. I took the bedroom suit we had purchased with my last bonus. Bob took the pool table that we purchased with money he had earned from side jobs. And honestly, even though I'm a musician at heart, the CD collection mostly meant more to him than me. So I let him go through it and pick out for me things he either didn't want or wanted me to have more than he wanted to keep them. He was very fair. Let's see, I got to keep the Prince and Steely Dan boxed sets along with many others I cherished. So I was pretty happy with that. I think he couldn't bear the thought of anyone not having music. It's very important to him. Or maybe he just didn't care that much for the ones he gave me.

I rather stupidly divided up minor things like our matching glassware and dish sets. I don't know what I was thinking other than that we both needed to live and would need the basics. But dividing up a matched set of dishes was really dumb. I even (for some ridiculous reason) kept half of a set of monogrammed towels with our initials on them. What the heck was I going to do with those? Display them? And they were a wedding gift! Geez, those really should have just been given to charity.

Looking back on it, I'm glad we hadn't acquired a lot of valuable stuff by that point, which kept the complications and arguments to a minimum.

Now on to the two remaining substantial items – the business Bob co-owned, and my 401K. I think technically I and his business partner's wife were listed as the owners of the business for tax purposes or something. But I had no active role other than opinions any spouse would offer. I had a 401K that had been partially funded by my employer. Bob had no retirement at that time. What to do?

At one point, I wanted to discuss a payout to me for part of the business since I had supported us financially when the business was getting started. However, it still wasn't producing a great deal of profit, and Bob had not been able to sock away any extra savings from it to position him to buy me out. I, on the other hand, had this 401K in which I was 100% vested. I guess a little selfishly at first, I felt that was mine. I had worked hard to earn that money giving up countless weekends and working late nights over long stretches of time. And if I wasn't going to get anything from the business, why should he get anything from my work? As we discussed this topic, Bob said he felt the 401K had built to where it was because of our joint earnings in all but a couple of years during his start up. The business he owned had more debt than equity, and it was his only means of immediate income. So putting it at risk created a whole other boatload of concerns for me around what might become of my son's standard of living. It just didn't work. I didn't want to drag it out just to see that hard-earned money sitting in my 401K end up in the hands of divorce attorneys. So I conceded on any rights to the business and split the retirement funds with Bob.

That pretty much settled our finances as far as the divorce went. And oh, by the way, unless you have more complicated assets than I've lain out above, be wary of attorneys who want to charge you thousands for this service. I provided my attorney with a spreadsheet that showed how all of our assets would be split. He proceeded to charge me (or rather, attempted to charge me) an exorbitant amount for his "time and effort." And I proceeded to pay him much less as a settlement, which, in my opinion, was still more than he had actually earned working on my case.

To be clear, for many people, it is probably a good idea to seek the advice of a financial advisor on splitting assets to make sure you, your children, and even extended family members are protected. In our case, I was the meticulous keeper of all of our finances having worked in the financial industry for years. And since Bob did trust me on financial matters, he was able to rely on the information I provided without question. Only you can judge whether or not this arrangement would work for you.

---

After we decided how to divide our assets, we had to move on to the painful business of deciding how our son's time would be split between us. Among all of the emotion of it, we had to distill it into legal terms to be included with our divorce decree. In the next chapter, I take you through our decision to go with joint custody complimented by a Shared Parenting Agreement, what that does and doesn't mean legally, and how this arrangement evolved over the years.

## *Chapter 2*
## *Shared Parenting: It's Not a Competition*

Of course, the most important decision we had to make with regard to our future lives as co-parents was how we would split our time with our son, Ian. Again, Bob's words "You're going to miss half of his life Teresa!" replayed in my head over and over again cutting through my soul each time I allowed the thought to enter. I talked to a few friends who were divorced to ask what their arrangements were. Mind you, since we were in our early 30s, many of our friends hadn't even married yet much less had kids or gotten divorced. So I had few people close enough to me to ask. There was the typical arrangement of the State of Ohio (common in many other states as well) which the majority of people still defaulted to, probably only because it was easier than taking the time and energy to discuss the situation with your soon-to-be-ex. That would require communicating with one another after all – the very reason many end up in divorce to begin with. So the default arrangement works like this: The mother is granted full custody of the child or children with the father getting *visitation* every other weekend and Wednesday evening from 6-9pm.

For me, the word *visitation* just pisses me off. It is so negative, evoking visions of either prisons or hospitals. It is not an appropriate term to associate with the hopefully happy time a father spends with his children. And the allowance of time? I was heartbroken when I thought about taking that much time away from Ian and his dad. I just couldn't do that.

For those who opted for arrangements other than the default, one option was the six months in one house and six months in another approach. No way was I going to do that. I would rather die than be apart from my son for 6 months at a stretch – even now that he is 25 years old!

Then a friend told me about "Shared Parenting." Now, what follows isn't a legal definition. So please consult an attorney. But the general idea is that you really are sharing the parental experience and responsibilities. Many do a week on / week off arrangement where one parent has the kids Sunday to Sunday and then they trade off. My friend who had this arrangement with his ex decided to modify this to a Friday-to-Friday arrangement. That way, they could start the weekend off happy to see their kids rather than spend Sunday dreading they were leaving. As a bonus, everyone could get ready to start their work or school week without the added turbulence of switching locations that evening. This sounded pretty good to both of us. So Bob and I went with a Friday-to-Friday arrangement, although we did make one more modification.

I simply could not come to terms with not seeing my then six-year-old boy for seven solid days at a time. So I suggested a mid-week switch. Once we moved to separate homes, we made a conscious choice (which I'll talk about more in Chapter 4 – Living in Two Homes) to live within a half-mile of one another. Since we lived so close, the back and forth this required was pretty easy to pull off. Yes, our residential choices were already about to pay dividends. So either

## Happily Divorced

Tuesday or Wednesday each week, Ian would go to the opposite parent's house to spend the night. He would then return to the other house for the remainder of the week. As I usually became uncontrollably weepy by Monday night due to separation anxiety since Friday, we opted for Tuesday during most of the time we maintained the midweek swap.

When Ian got into middle school and was involved in a few activities, we all mutually agreed to forgo the midweek swap. Sure, we had duplicated a lot of things. But not everything. So it was a daily challenge to make sure the soccer gear and band equipment – especially the small yet significant stuff to a $7^{th}$ grader – was in the right house at precisely the moment he needed or wanted it. And let's be honest, at least from my experience, most guys and boys don't check if they have everything they need for any activity until about five minutes before they actually need it. As such, there was the inevitable panic that would set in for both child and parent when either realized a mere ten minutes before the start of practice or, worse yet, game arrival time, that the only set of shin guards for soccer were at the other parent's house and that parent was not at home.

Thankfully due to our carefully orchestrated arrangement, we had even found a way to deal with these last minute snafus, which seems like yet another obvious solution but not one everyone is either comfortable with or thinks about. We gave each other a means of accessing the other parent's home either with a key or using the key pad on the garage. Now you have to have a pretty high level of trust in your ex-spouse to literally give him or her the keys to your home, and granted, this isn't for everyone. But if your only hesitation isn't a trust issue but rather an unnecessary belief that this isn't appropriate or "people just don't do that," you're just making life harder on yourself and your child for no good reason. Some might also say that you could just deal with the issue by giving the child the access, and of course, you could. However, let's be real. If the child has the key or code, then the ex-spouse has the key or code. Going further, if the other parent is forbidden from accessing the ex-spouse's home and the child is young, there are at least a couple of situations you could encounter, some of which we did.

There were times Ian would go into his dad's house to pick up something he needed ABSOLUTELY NOW and in full-blown panic, of course, couldn't find it. Mom (or dad) was there to calm the situation down and help him focus on finding this item that, to him at that moment, was the difference between life being perfectly fine and the impending end of happiness as we know it. On the more extreme end of the spectrum, one that fortunately we did *not* encounter was what if the child goes into the home without the parent and something awful happens? Maybe he injures himself as he climbs a piece of furniture to grab something. Or maybe he turns something on, that if left unattended would cause a fire after we've left. Sure, we try to teach our kids how to avoid these situations. But everyone can make a mistake, and one of our biggest responsibilities as parents is ensuring the safety of our children. So you have to consider that a young child is not mature enough to be saddled with so much responsibility without as much as a second set of more mature eyes looking behind him in such situations. At least that's my belief.

In addition to our week-to-week and mid-week swap arrangement, both Ian and I and Ian and his dad spoke on the phone every day for several more years to further perpetuate the parental bond daily during our absence.

## *Happily Divorced*

One final consideration which we included in our arrangement that I would encourage you to discuss with the other parent is the distance from which the two of you can live from one another. Some parents agree to reside within the same school district, which can be a pretty small geographic radius but does ensure that both parents reside in the school district where their child attends school and therefore allows for a variety of added conveniences besides proximity including, in many cases, bus transportation. We agreed to a maximum distance of 45 miles that we could live apart from one another. I had friends who had to drive hours each way to trade the kids with the co-parent. And this made it far more difficult to attend school functions and other activities in which the child was involved local to one parent. Of course, there were other parents who took job transfers in other states making anything other than long absences from one parent or the other all but inevitable. So our living arrangement seemed to guard against these circumstances that just didn't seem tenable to either of us.

I can't express here how much this arrangement of close proximity, week-to-week shared parenting, the midweek swap, and shared access to each other's home contributed to a smoother, more relaxed, and happier existence. But hopefully, this gives you some idea of what can be gained from considering it. If you have younger children and are in the throes of deciding on your child-parent visitation, or as I like to call it, *shared time*, I would highly recommend trying it out to see if it works for you.

---

Since Bob and I separated in July, it wasn't long before the school year was upon us, and Ian was set to start his academic journey in the fall just as we were coming through all of the painful decisions that go into the divorce process. Unfortunately, we would now have to navigate the school system as divorced parents and figure out how to not let our decision set Ian up for difficulties as he started kindergarten. We'd also have to expose our failure as a married couple to this government institution as it starts with the enrollment paperwork and only one place to list your child's residence.

## Chapter 3
## School Days: Parents & Teachers Take Note

One of the first things we had to encounter as recently-divorced parents was the school system. Ian entered kindergarten about 2 months after we separated. You would have thought divorce was a brand new concept. Everything from emergency information forms to grade cards was designed to accommodate parents who lived at the same residence. And this was 1999!

As I was designated as the residential parent in our arrangement, everything school related was based on my address. Nothing was ever mailed to Bob. And this is where demonstrating both sensibility and kindness begins. I know plenty of divorced parents who struggle with this

*Ian coming home after the first day of kindergarten*

most basic right. I never hesitated for a second. I assumed Bob was entitled to all the same information about Ian's education as I was. How could I expect him to otherwise be a good parent? I had to remember what I wanted my son to have and what I wanted in a father for him. I always made sure Bob was offered the opportunity to purchase school pictures. And I made sure he got a copy of every grade card. The school didn't do this. I did! They, it seemed, never even thought of it as a service they should offer. This doesn't make any sense to me. I also don't understand mothers who refuse to consider how they might feel if they weren't even given the opportunity to get school pictures from one year of grade school. All too frequently, divorced fathers miss out on a lot. And this benefits no one. The father suffers. The child and father connection is weakened as the father receives less and less ongoing information about the child's evolution.

If you take this course and think you'll come out of it unscathed, I implore you to reconsider. Karma is a bitch you do NOT want to meet. Also, ask yourself how it could possibly benefit your child for his or her other parent to be denied information and experiences with them.

I remember the first night conference during which we met Ian's kindergarten teacher. We had separated about 6 weeks before. Of course, we both wanted to be there. So we did this crazy thing: we talked about it. Then we did another crazy thing. We agreed to both go and let the teacher know that even though we were divorcing, we weren't one of those dysfunctional couples who hate each other and yell all the time, which was a kind of interesting evolution since one of the reasons we split up was because of our incessant arguing. (We argued about everything from life philosophies to how to play a Euchre hand. God forbid I stray from Hoyle. Yep, divorce, or at least living separately, seemed to fix our dysfunction as a couple – and as Euchre partners. Oh, the irony!)

As we squeezed ourselves into tiny little kindergartener desks, I made my pronouncement to the new teacher, Mrs. Joseph, that we were divorcing but that we get along, and she would not have any problems with us. As it turned out, this was Mrs. Joseph's first year teaching *anywhere*. So she was probably simultaneously concerned, skeptical, and relieved. Ian had this teacher for two years, and as we approached the end of the second year, Mrs. Joseph, disbelieving or not, pulled me aside to tell me not only how special our little boy is (yep, Mom already knows that) but also how lucky he is to have two parents who work so hard to make this whole divorce thing into as positive an experience as possible for him. Now, those two words, "divorce" and "positive," don't normally appear in the same sentence. But two years into our positive co-parenting approach and people around us were beginning to see the effect it was having on our son. And he was feeling it too!

## *A Son's Perspective*

I feel the need to comment here, but not so much about school. See, school was pretty normal for me, as far as I know. There was nothing extra-difficult or different about school that was directly caused by my parents' separation except leaving school supplies at the wrong house. Luckily, my parents were smart enough and mature enough to make the decision to live within a stone's throw of each other throughout my schooling, so the supplies problem (or anything else I forgot at the wrong house) could be alleviated pretty easily.

The main thing I want to point out is how my parents' relationship did actually move in a positive direction when they got divorced. The year or so leading up to the divorce, there was a lot of yelling. Things never got violent, but the arguments got heated, and the words got heavy. My parents would even literally get into a yelling match over clothes or the weather or whatever useless topic one can find to argue about. They were both arguing to prove the other wrong, to prove themselves right, and for no other purpose—which, by the way, is an inherent issue I've found in humans. From all-caps trolling matches in Facebook comments to Capitol Hill, people argue for the sake of arguing, not to find real solutions.

Anyway, once my parents were fully separated, living different lives in different homes, but still raising the same child, something amazing happened: my parents started working together to find solutions. They weren't around each other enough to bicker about nothing; if they were conversing, it was important and needed to be discussed like adults. For whatever reason, the evolution our family took allowed my parents to do this. And it relieved a lot of stress on this guy, too!

---

As Ian noted above, one of the decisions we made that made things less stressful for him and us was our choice to live in close proximity to one another. In the next chapter, I'll share more details on how this one decision made life so much easier for us as parents living separately.

## Chapter 4
## *Living in Two Homes: A Family Guide*

When we decided a mere two years after we married that neither of us was keeping the home we had built, I looked at many neighborhoods, many homes, and a couple of other school districts. Fortunately, I made enough to afford to buy a home on my own. So I didn't have to consider apartments. Bob, too, could independently swing a home mortgage and expenses. We would both have to downgrade on the luxuries slightly and not have as much money left over for extras after the mortgage, for sure. But we could provide a comfortable home – actually two – for our son.

I decided to stay in the exceptional school district we were in, and I got lucky enough to find another home in the same neighborhood about a quarter mile away on a street that I knew had several boys Ian's age. It was on a *cul de sac* and backed up to a ravine. No neighbors behind us and plenty of woods and even a stream. While the home was smaller, the lot was an upgrade, something that eased my pain of losing our other home that we had built.

Bob, being in the building industry himself, chose to build a home that was in an up-and-coming neighborhood through a thin line of trees and across one main road directly behind my house. It was only about a quarter-mile as the crow flies. So I knew as Ian got older, he'd eventually be able to go between our two houses on foot or by bike.

Of course, something I didn't think about as much was how much easier living so close made things for everyone. Since we were in the same school district, there were some years when Ian could take the bus from and to either home. And when that wasn't the case, Ian's dad was so close, he could drop him off to me in the morning since he worked earlier and I could put him on the bus. This gave me a chance each day to see my son before school – yet another strategy for regaining some of that "half of his life" I was missing. Then there was the ongoing transfer of clothes, toys, sports equipment, homework, and music instruments in between homes. When Ian was young, I or his father packed his stuff up. As he got older, Ian started doing it himself. Whether it was us or him, there were hundreds of items over the years that had to be retrieved from one house or another. We both got frustrated from time to time with Ian forgetting stuff, but we both acknowledged that it couldn't be easy living in two places at once. I had never done it and was sure given my crappy memory that I'd have been running back and forth in between houses at least daily and maybe even hourly to get a particular jacket, book, or stuffed animal.

To minimize this madness, we bought duplicates of some of the main items. We also used this strategy to offer roughly the same experience at each home. We even bought Ian the same bed. As much as Bob and I had competed during our marriage to win every conversation, neither of us was interested in seeing the other one lose in the parenting game. We had finally found a motivation to be nice to one another. So we purchased two swing sets, two bikes, plenty of clothes for both houses, and two drum kits. Oh, there had to be two drum kits! Otherwise, one of us would have never seen our child or we would have been stuck carting that set back and forth for years to come. As it turned out, when Ian reached fifth grade and created his first rock band, we did end up carting around the drums a lot. Except rather than it being between homes, it was from the house to a show and back. And yes, we both helped load in and load out. When Ian got big enough to carry the drums himself, we chose solidarity and both declared our days as roadies over.

Also with adolescence came some other benefits to the close living arrangement we had chosen. Since there was literally only one house blocking my view of Bob's backyard from my back door, I was comfortable allowing Ian to walk between our homes since I could watch him walk most of the way and his dad could see him on the other side when I lost sight. This was very handy not only when items were forgotten at the other home but also worked out quite well during the middle-school years when Ian got along much better with the kids on Bob's street than on mine. This was great. I never wanted Ian to prefer one home over another because of our choices. And I never wanted him to be bummed out that he had to go to another home and leave his friends behind for a week. Oh sure, there was some of this, especially when our inter-district boundaries were different and the kids in Bob's neighborhood ended up at a different middle-school and high school. In general, though, I think this arrangement's benefits went a long way to improve the circumstances of our separated family. But it didn't happen by accident. We chose to make it happen this way.

If you are divorcing and contemplating your post-marriage living arrangement, I do have a couple of suggestions for you. First, I know it isn't always possible or the best choice to live within a quarter mile of each other as Bob and I did. However, I will say I think it behooves you to live close enough to not make it extraordinarily difficult for your child and your ex-spouse to spend time together. I personally think walking distance IS the best choice if you want the optimal shared-parenting arrangement. But at least make it a short drive if it has to be that way. And try to stay in the same school district so that both parents can feel more connected to their child's academic community. Additionally, paying taxes to the school district where the child attends does tend to make a parent feel they have more of a vested interest in the decisions made by that institution.

Whatever you decide on, I highly recommend including a proximity parameter within your divorce decree stating that you both agree to live within a particular mileage of one another until the child turns eighteen. I know this can be career limiting for some. You may have to curtail upward mobility until your child is older. Be careful of your perspective on this one, though, and also remember the Golden Rule here. Would you want the other parent to live so far away that it will place a burden on you to accommodate your ex's parental rights? Worse yet, if your ex is the "custodial parent" – the one designated as the primary residence for the child – how would you feel if your ex up and moved a hundred or even a thousand miles away with your child in the pursuit of a career completely disregarding your rights and your child's rights to have you in their lives on a consistent basis?

Life is about choices. You have a very important one to make in this regard. And granted, you may not feel that you have to establish a legal commitment to distance parameters now. But if your child is young, so much can change. And you don't want such an important matter to be left entirely to the idea that you will always have a positive relationship with your spouse. You never know who might influence your ex or you in the future. Even with this parameter agreed to legally, of course, if a desperate situation arises and you have to revisit the parameter to which you agreed, it really is no different than having to address the situation without the agreement. The legal agreement simply provides the other parent with some leverage or even recourse should things change this way, which would force the other parent to consider his or her decisions against possible legal penalties.

Finally, I'll add that with all the good things that came from Bob and me living that short quarter mile from each other, one thing was a bit uncomfortable at first: Bob's view of my driveway every time he pulled out of his neighborhood. While this discomfort did pass fairly quickly as we moved on with our lives and relationships, his ability to see other cars in my drive AND know how long they may have been there made for some awkward moments!

---

At this point, you might be asking yourself how two people who were able to reconcile differences rather easily after divorce couldn't seem to get it together to save their marriage. It's a fair question, and when you read about the cracks in our relationship that eventually developed into an irreconcilable chasm of differences, you may very well end up mad at one or both of us. But if you think that passions played out as hobbies in one's life are trivial, you may want to consider how you have felt when anyone ever told you that you couldn't do or have that thing in your life that makes you feel truly alive. It is dangerous to discount what is important to those you love. What may not seem like a big deal to you may be a monumental sacrifice to give up for another. If only we could have tried to see things through the other person's eyes. If only we could have given more focus to what we already had.

## *Chapter 5*
## *Motorcycles, Boats, & Conflicts: Oh My!*

If I had to pick a point of contention within our marriage that changed the course of our future, I would pin it to decisions that revolved around motorcycles and boats. Maybe this sounds lame to some people – that our marriage hinged on two inanimate objects – two of our hobbies. But these two things are more than just inanimate objects and hobbies to each of us. They add "living" to our lives.

Bob and I are passionate people with strong opinions and a commitment to living life to the fullest. Some people may be okay just cruising through life on autopilot. Not us. We both want to experience life and drink in the pleasures of being human. It is fleeting, after all. Our strong passions for life could have been a great asset to our marriage, and I'd say early on they were, as we shared many common interests.

For starters, Bob loves motorcycles and I like them well enough. I love boating and Bob likes boating well enough — or at least he did. On our first date, we road on his motorcycle together. Later on, Bob introduced me to waterskiing. For many years, we enjoyed both of these activities together. But as time marched on, our passions began to diverge and became a point of contention. Bob had to become a

Harley rider. And I had to become a boat owner. We just had to. But each got in the way of the other, and this is when the trouble started.

When Ian was about 2 years old, I got a substantial raise at my job. I wanted to buy a boat that we could all enjoy together as Ian got older. Bob thought it was a good time to buy his first Harley. Back in the mid-90s, not only were Harleys quality motorcycles, they were also actually very good investments. You couldn't even purchase a new one without getting on a waiting list first. Finally, with my new income and Bob's business generating a reasonable salary for him, we could have afforded either a boat or a motorcycle, albeit a modest selection of whichever one we chose. But we certainly couldn't afford both. It seemed we had a decision to make. Would we buy the Harley that Bob wanted or the Mastercraft ski boat that I dreamed of owning?

A few months into my new job and income, Bob *announced* to me that he had put himself on the wait list for a Harley. What? I was pissed. *We* had not agreed on this. How were we going to enjoy a motorcycle with a two- year old? Three people do not fit on a motorcycle! They could, however, all fit comfortably in a boat! To make use of the motorcycle together, Bob suggested that we could get his mom to watch Ian when we went on the bike. I could not see me enjoying that experience at all. I had waited too long to have a child and wasn't interested in leaving Ian at home so that I could become a biker. I made my case for the boat. Still, *we* proceeded with the purchase of Bob's first Harley.

As Ian's third birthday approached, I was ecstatic with motherhood. Yet, I couldn't quite shake an undeniable sense I was leaving some part of my life *unlived*. It felt like I was conceding the decisions that determined what type of life I would have to others. The type of career I'd pursue, the friends I'd keep, and the hobbies I'd participate in were guided primarily by Bob's preferences and priorities. And he didn't even know that he was in control. After all, I was not a wilting flower personality. Ultimately, I made the choices I made. I could have chosen a different career. I could have made more friends of my own. I could have saved more money and found a way for us to buy a boat. Bob never tried to stop me from doing anything. He simply was better at designing his life and then executing his plan. Oh the irony of that last statement given my career as a project manager. The one project I was failing to manage was my own life.

In some cases, this actually worked out for the best. For instance, when Bob and I got together, I had drifted from my passion for singing. When early on in our relationship, he discovered I had a talent for it, he encouraged me to get back to singing. He even hooked me up with some guys he was friends with who had a band to jumpstart the idea. It was clear to me then and even more so now that Bob did want me to be happy and live my passion. But whether it was true or not, I doubted Bob would really concede on certain designs he had for our lives that conflicted with mine. Ultimately, rather than finding a way to clearly communicate to him my desires and express why these things were important to me, I eventually felt the necessity to bow out of our relationship.

A few years before Ian was born, Bob developed a circuit of friends who owned ski boats and were avid water skiers. They taught me to ski, and I fell in love with the sport. I loved everything about being on the water – the beautiful scenery, the rev of the boat engine, the warmth of the sun beating down on my skin, making great memories with friends, and the speed of flying across the wake on one ski. Truly, waterskiing was the first sport I felt reasonably good at. It was freeing. For me, boating offered a uniquely liberating experience – exhilarating and relaxing at the same time. Truth be told, Bob was actually a much better water-skier than me back in the day. Being the competitive person I am, this just motivated me to get better, to keep up. However, to improve, I wanted – dare I say needed? – more rope time. So we went with friends as often as we could. We started going on houseboat trips to Lake Cumberland where we could ski from morning until night. I looked forward all year every year to those houseboat trips and being back on the lake. As soon as we got in our cars to leave the lake each year, I looked fondly upon my return. Then in the fall of '97, our boating friends Bill and Crystal, who also happened to be Harley riders, bought a house on a river in Columbus, in the ski zone, no less! It was awesome because we enjoyed each other's company, and they were very gracious in sharing their amenities with us. We brought Ian, had cookouts, and definitely water-skied our butts off.

As spring '98 approached, it was time to plan the annual houseboat trip, which usually took place in June. When I inquired about the plan, Bob explained to me that he and Bill had been talking and that they really wanted for the four of us to forego the houseboat trip this *one* year and instead go to Milwaukee for the Harley Davidson 95$^{th}$ Anniversary celebration. He talked about how fun it would be with thousands of bikes and a new destination to explore. He presented it as a choice, but somehow I felt a *no* was only going to be met with a fierce argument. So as I thought about challenging this suggestion, I tried to see it as a compromise. It wasn't a houseboat trip but it was only one year we'd miss it. This would be a different type of memorable experience. Didn't it make sense to mix things up a bit? Have some variety in our lives? We had never taken a trip on the Harley in the two years since Bob had purchased it, yet we had went on a couple houseboat trips in that same time period. So I agreed. But just for this *one* year.

## Happily Divorced

The next spring, again it was time to plan the houseboat trip, and I had heard no talk of it. So I asked Bob, and he *announced* to me that this year, he and Bill were instead going to go to Sturgis for their annual Harley bikers' rally. What? Wait! I thought we were only skipping *one* year at the lake. That was the deal. As I pictured riding out to Sturgis, South Dakota and spending my precious vacation time amongst bikers while my beloved lake did without me, I suggested that I may not be interested in doing that. Oh, no problem, Bob said. Sturgis was going to be a guys-only trip. No women allowed. Really? How do you think that went over? I couldn't believe it. When I voiced my opposition to this plan and reminded him of our one-year retreat from the lake, Bob was incensed. "What's the big deal?" he said. "We can ski on the river anytime we want with Bill and Crystal." What? That is NOT THE SAME! It wasn't the lake NOR a houseboat trip!!! And it wasn't the agreement we had made the year before. It started to become apparent to me that Bob's priorities and mine were at odds, and I felt like I was always the one conceding my desires.

Faced with missing a second year in a row at my beloved lake, I asked Bob if he minded if I tried to find another houseboat trip to go on by myself. He said he didn't care. So this is what we had come to . . . separate vacations. Still, Bob saying he didn't care relieved me of any guilt in the matter, and I proceeded to find a houseboat trip to join. I knew of at least one other friend who was going on a trip and promptly made a call to ask her if there was room for me. Of course there was. So both out of spite and desire, I packed my bags and was on a houseboat on Lake Cumberland in about three weeks. Bob's decision to plan a vacation without me to Sturgis and my decision to go on a houseboat trip without him would change the course of our future as husband and wife.

*Teresa Harlow*

I was so giddy the morning of the trip I couldn't contain myself. It was like I was overwhelmed with a sense of freedom. FINALLY, I was deciding how to live my life rather than feeling as if someone else was dictating it to me. I ended up riding down with a friend of the friend who planned the trip along with a few others, none of whom I knew all that well. On the way there, I felt a connection developing between me and the guy who was driving – not as a love interest (at least not at that point) – but rather as someone who shared my passion for boating, my philosophy about life, and who was excessively easy to talk to. He got me! Bob used to understand me, but somewhere along the way, he stopped getting me and just became critical of me. Why wasn't I more this or less that? To be fair, I, too, had become resentful and mean-spirited in our interactions toward the end of our marriage.

This new friend and I proceeded to spend endless hours talking about everything including family, our academic backgrounds, our careers, and of course, our mutual dream of living on the water. Oh, and did I mention he owned a Mastercraft ski boat?!?! As the four days on the lake passed, we also ventured into turbulent waters, quite literally, while discussing the current state of my marriage. As we talked, I felt this urgency building inside of me that if I didn't choose to start living my life my way right then and there, I was going to be one of those people lying on my death bed suffocated by regret. It weighed heavily on me. And I was so disappointed that Bob, so focused on his own desires, couldn't see I was missing out on *my* life. So, while I gave a lot of thought during that trip as to what my life could be as someone choosing my own path, I gave little thought to what it wouldn't be, what it could no longer be.

## Happily Divorced

I returned from the houseboat trip and was only home about three days when I announced to Bob that I wanted a divorce. And that was that. Bob and I split up over motorcycles and boats.

Of course, this isn't exactly true. We didn't split up *over* these things. We split up because we both stopped treating each other as we wanted to be treated. We stopped caring about each other's desires and wanting each other to be happy. We had both become consumed with our individual dreams and forgot to listen to each other. We forgot about our little dream family we had created. Bob seemed to me to want his boyish freedom to roam the country with his buddies. I wanted the freedom of skiing behind a boat any time I chose. I wanted to introduce my son to the boating experience as I'm sure Bob wanted to indoctrinate Ian in the ways of the Harley rider. In the end, though, it was really about each of us choosing our own life path, not one that was thrust upon us.

After our divorce, Bob upgraded his Harley to a nicer model and enjoyed plenty of free time riding with the guys. I got my boat, more rope time, and a whole new group of friends – friends that liked me for me, not because I was Bob's wife. Friends that shared my love of

boating and the lake. I know neither of us regrets having these things in our lives now. They are the fabric of who we each have become. But it's unfortunate we couldn't figure out how to make room for both of these things in our family.

Ian, on the verge of turning six years old when Bob and I separated, liked, but I wouldn't say *loved*, boating. He tolerated it and liked the swimming but didn't really get into watersports until middle school. Then he discovered wakeboarding and grew to like that a lot. As soon as Ian was old enough to hang on to his dad securely, he road with Bob on the back of his bike. I'm sure he enjoyed that just as I did as a child riding on my dad's Honda with him. While it pains me that Ian couldn't enjoy these things with us together, I'm glad he has gotten to experience both of our passions, just as we've shared in his passion for music. And maybe our divorce was the only way that was ever going to happen.

If you and your spouse are struggling because of conflicting desires, I think it is key to understand your partner's passions and support them. Nothing will kill a relationship more quickly than denying someone those dreams. If you don't know what those dreams are, you had better ask. If you think you know her dreams, you better make sure you're right and are paying attention. If those dreams conflict with yours, you must work through it. Don't leave it to chance and don't make assumptions. We know what that does.

This doesn't mean you should allow your partner's dreams to keep you from living yours. If someone loves you and wants to be with you enough, make sure he or she knows what your dreams are. You can't be pissed that your partner killed your dreams if he or she didn't know what they were. And for God's sake, make sure they're listening. If your partner doesn't work with you to help you achieve your dreams, or worse, stands *in* your way of them, you're probably headed for trouble or already in it. Likewise, if you can't come to terms with the dreams your partner holds and find room for compromise, you're going to struggle. Best to move on from the relationship because one or both of you will always be haunted by your unlived dreams.

---

While I did begin another relationship as Bob and mine was ending, I had lingering doubts about my decision for many months. I grieved the loss of my traditional family. The time I spent without my son was excruciating. What if all of this was just a big mistake? Could we try again? Could I go back?

## *Chapter 6*
## *Reconciliation: Nice But No Dice*

When Bob and I split up, I was at war with myself for quite some time. On the one hand, I just didn't feel like Bob and I were destined to spend eternity together as husband and wife. There was too much anger, too little care, too much selfishness on both our parts, and too few passionate moments between us. I wanted the fairytale. I wanted someone who genuinely liked me just the way I am. I didn't want to compete with my partner in the course of every conversation. I really felt Bob wanted and should be with someone who had a softer, gentler demeanor than I had or desired to have. I also wanted Bob to have what he wanted . . . because he was my friend and a really good man who deserved true love. I didn't feel like I was capable of giving him that. So I felt I had to release him so that we could both find what we wanted in a relationship and live that dream. I wanted Ian to see that, too. I didn't want him to settle on a life partner that fell short of his desires.

But that's not to say I felt I was settling when Bob and I met and married. I really did love Bob and saw a relationship for us. And at first, it seemed we had the right formula. On our first date, we road on his motorcycle, ate Italian food, and played pool. We liked similar music, enjoyed similar activities, and shared the same values. And we were both sarcastic as hell. So we got each other. Of course, that last attribute ultimately backfired in our faces as sarcasm gets old after a while and you just want your partner to talk nice to you and tell you how right and awesome you are.

When I came back from that fateful houseboat trip on which I met a new man who showed the promise of many of the things I felt were lacking in my current situation, I didn't pause to think about what I'd be giving up. I should have. Maybe. But I didn't. I felt like I was a car with no reverse gear and I had been heading toward that moment for a long time. I couldn't back up just because Bob finally realized the situation was serious. I had been telling him for two years we were going to end up divorced if things continued as they had. But he seemed to think I was joking, or maybe it was the product of all that sarcastic history between us.

So I forged ahead straight into this relationship with a man I just met. I told Bob I wanted a divorce, and then the next day received a call from my frantic friend, Jessie, who told me this new guy had a past and shared what she knew with me. She said I needed to know he wasn't perfect. She pleaded with me to reconsider my decision to leave Bob and to stay away from the new guy. I was shocked and devastated! How could I have misjudged the situation so horribly? Maybe she was mistaken. Maybe his past problems were no longer an issue. I was with him most of the time during our trip and never saw any of the behaviors she claimed. I prosecuted the case in my biased head and concluded it was a non-issue and that if it became one, it was one I was going to help him fix. Yes, I was going to fix him. Sound familiar, girls?

Now, you may be asking why I didn't try to "fix" Bob – invest my time there. Well, I had already concluded that I wasn't the girl who was going to be able to do that. Bob had no desire to be fixed nor any thought that he should be. Of course, in a way, he was right . . . if only he had been with the right partner.

As I stepped into this other relationship, I was swept up in that "new love" feeling you get where everything is rainbows and butterflies and you only see the good in everything the other person does. I was also swept up in the agonizing loss of my family, and it put a black cloud over everything else, even the new love feeling. Add to that Bob pleading with me to not do this to him and Ian, and there was enough pressure to cause my head to explode. Something had to give. Neither of these relationships was going to survive all this.

The new guy, Steve, did seem to really care about me. He told me that he only wanted me if he could have me free of the black cloud. So he suggested I make sure this was what I really wanted and suggested I give Bob and my family another chance. I was reluctant because honestly, for the first time in a long time, I was enjoying the company of a man. I asked him how long he thought I should give it, and he suggested a month or two. A month or two? From my perspective, I had already given it years since first contemplating the thought of divorce. I couldn't bear the thought of investing more time and losing the possibility of this new relationship. I just knew I would figure out whether this was a viable path much more quickly. We agreed to a two-week hiatus from each other so that I would have the distance from him to think more clearly – or so I thought.

I shared the plan with Bob, who was very happy to hear I was willing to try. Yep, after two years of me warning him of this fate, he now felt like it was time we do everything in our power to not lose our marriage. Why, oh why did he wait until we were this far gone to fully commit to working on it? Had he thought he already had? Had I missed his previous attempts blinded by anger and deafened by our spiteful words toward one another? In any case, I was going to at least try to give it my finest effort. We both agreed it was best to not tell Ian about our plan. He was too young to understand how complicated this was, and we didn't want to get his hopes up just to disappoint him yet again with more bad news.

Bob asked me out on a "date" early into the two weeks. We went to dinner, I think, and then either to the Funny Bone, a local comedy club, or Shadow Box Theatre. The fact I can't remember probably speaks volumes about the chances I gave it. That isn't to say I didn't try to give it my all that night. Just for whatever reason in that moment on that night, I felt like I was on a date with a friend rather than my husband or romantic partner. It really hurt because I so much wanted a switch to flip on inside me that would take me back to the magical moments of our early relationship and allow me to fall back in love with my husband and the father of my child. Bob was a complete gentleman the entire night and tried very hard to be the right guy for me, too. But I just couldn't feel it, and it broke my heart. I was going to have to say goodbye to our marriage and the family as we knew it. I berated myself for that failed performance as a wife for years to come. I was a failure as a wife and really didn't even deserve to be given a second chance; yet, I pissed it away as if it was nothing.

The night following our "date" I went to karaoke at a local bar close to home with friends. As I sulked in my failure feeling very alone, Steve walked in. He had found out where I was through friends, I guess, and breached our distance agreement. Bob was furious when I told him this the following day, and he blamed Steve for our failure to reconcile. I begged him to see this for what it was – *our* failure and more aptly at the moment, *my* failure. After our conversation, I promptly called Steve to inform him I was choosing to be with him and we called off the hiatus officially about a week early.

Bob and I moved on from that moment and revisited reconciliation at least once more a few months later. I was once again on hiatus from Steve as we had discovered what I felt may be a deal-breaking difference in our future dreams – the promise of having more children. I had never intended to have only one child, and I wanted to give Ian a sibling. However, Steve had quite a different opinion due to the custody battle with his ex for his daughter, which he was still embroiled in some 9 years later. Yeah, I get why he may have had apprehensions. So we parted while I further contemplated if giving up my dream of having a second child was something I could come to terms with.

In the meantime, Bob started dating a younger girl, whom I concluded was probably not right for him. Why I felt I was in a position to judge, I have no idea. But she just struck me as too immature for him and maybe shallow. She did have a nice figure and was very pretty. So I could see the reasons he might be attracted to her. Yet, I had to believe there must be more to her than that since I knew Bob was not a shallow person. He would not continue to see someone based only on looks.

One day, when he was at my house picking Ian up, we were standing in the kitchen. I remember it well; I felt a resurgence of an old familiar feeling similar to the attraction I had for Bob in our early days. He had a glow about him void of any anger or anxiety for the first time in a long time. I asked him how things were going and took a deep breath as I awaited his response. He said, "Really well, actually." My heart sank as I realized that now Bob may be the one who was unable to find a reverse gear. He asked me why I looked so distraught, and I shared with him that I was really hoping he'd say they were through and that maybe we were in a position now to try again. He was shocked to hear this but was willing to consider it.

Once again, Bob and I set out to attempt reconciliation, and again we didn't share our plan with Ian. We proceeded to go to a Queensryche rock concert together. Dammit! Again, I felt like I was on a date with a friend. Steve was still in my head. But I was having this ever-building feeling of dread about us.

There was something not quite right. He rarely had a job but always had cash. While I was at his house one day, the cable company showed up at his door to disconnect service due to no payment. His finances were a weird mystery that made me very uncomfortable. And he was pretty much a complete slob around the house in spite of a lot of free time. You'd think this, combined with the earlier warning from my friend, might have prompted me to exit that relationship right there for good. But still I returned to him, conceding my desire for more children and more determined than ever to fix whatever problems there might be. At least I had that loving feeling again.

By this point, Steve and I had introduced our kids to one another, and they got along like two peas in a pod. They were so happy together. His daughter was enjoying spending time with her dad finally after years of her mother withholding visitation. Ian was enjoying the closest thing I could give him to a sibling and just seemed to love Kimberly. So while red flags told me to exit the situation, the tangled web I had woven coupled with the good stuff Steve and I had such as our shared love of boating and ability to hang out for hours without ever criticizing each other kept me in this ill-fated relationship for another 3 years. By the eventual end of that relationship, Bob had met and married the new love of his life, Brandi. I couldn't be happier for him.

*Happily Divorced*

---

As Bob and I exited our union as husband and wife, the realization of all that I was losing started to sink in. My support system of family and friends was undergoing a major overhaul. I was suddenly a single mom with a house, a full-time job, no family within a thousand miles, and few friends to turn to for help. How was I going to survive?

I sunk into grief as I contemplated the loss of so many wonderful people in my life that had been there for me when I most needed them. Was I going to lose the love of Bob's mom and sister? Would they ever talk to me again? Had I really gained the so-called sanity I sought by redesigning my life or had the insanity just begun? I had a new man, a new house, and a boat. But what about my family?

## Chapter 7
## In Laws: If You Like Them, Keep Them!

Some people like their in-laws. Some hate them. And some simply tolerate them. I love Bob's family. Always have and always will. It's not because they are perfect. Who is? It's because they accept me even though I'm not perfect. They've also afforded me their forgiveness and have been there when I needed them. I've tried to give them the same in return. In times when I've been challenged by relationships with my own family, I have found comfort in the bonds created and sustained with my in-laws. How lucky I am!

Yet, let me be clear – I love my mom and dad even though they sometimes make me crazy for one reason or another. Whose doesn't? My mom and dad are two of the most genuine people on the planet. I have no doubt they are who they say they are and mean what they

*Teresa's Parents, Helen & Don*

say. They are honest, hard-working people who just want the best for their children. They've sacrificed much in their pursuit of that goal. It's taken me a long time to really appreciate the depth of the love they've given me. And certainly that was made more difficult by my decision to move back to Ohio from Houston when I was 20 years old, leaving my parents behind.

## *My Mother-in-Law*

Being on my own in Ohio, while even at a distance of 1,200 miles, my parents were there for me when I needed them. Yet, this distance has denied me the simple pleasures of enjoying casual family dinners, playing cards, or just having a cup of coffee together on a cold winter weekend morning.

When I met Bob's mom, I felt an instant connection with her. Sandy shared many similarities beyond her astrological sign, Sagittarius, with my mom – solid values, unwavering honesty, refreshing authenticity, and a mother's protective attitude toward her children, which she extended without hesitation to me.

*Bob with his mom (Teresa's Mother-in-law) Sandy, and Ian*

In effect, Sandy was my "local" mom. So while my parents lived far away, Sandy and her husband Dick, along with Bob's dad and stepmom, Charlotte, lived within a reasonable drive. This made it easy to join them for dinner, holidays, and other family gatherings both planned and spontaneous. And it never felt forced or awkward with the exception of the many times we arrived after we had fought in the car on the entire drive to their house.

## *My Sister-in-Law*

Bob's sister was still in high school when we first started dating. I remember attending an orchestra performance watching sister Debbie as she played First-Chair flute in the All-Columbus City Schools band. I was so proud of her. She was beautiful, very shy, kind, and what we referred to in the 80s as straight-laced. She also seemed to really enjoy having someone to call sister in her life. Through the years, we laughed and cried with Debbie as she graduated high school, lived with us

*Bob's sister (Teresa's Sister-in-law), Debbie with Ian*

while she attended college, broke up with boyfriends, and then eventually met and married the love of her life. In fact, Debbie and I were so close that I was the matron of honor in her wedding. This meant a lot to me since I didn't have a sister either and was never terribly good at keeping female friends. Of course, I thought I had ruined that friendship forever when only a month after her wedding, I announced my separation from her brother.

*Teresa Harlow*

## *A Child Among Us*

When our son, Ian, was born, the bond with Bob's family continued to grow – especially since Ian was the first grandchild in the family. He was showered with love and gifts enough for ten kids and enjoyed his "only grandchild" status for a long 7 years. For us, it meant we had eager babysitting options in Grandma and Aunt Debbie. This should have truly afforded us the alone time Bob and I needed to continue building a solid bond as husband and wife. Yet we didn't do that. We both were very good at focusing on Ian and being good parents. But somehow we couldn't get beyond our own egos enough to focus on being the best to each other. Problems in our marriage developed unchecked and eventually became a gulf of differences that we could not bridge.

## *Miss Independent?*

When I decided to divorce Bob, I was terrified of losing my much-loved "local family." What would become of me? They were the ones I celebrated most holidays and special occasions with. It was Sandy and Dick who shared in our joy as we watched Ian eat his first birthday cake, collect Easter eggs for the first time, and beat on his first drum kit. They were my local support in times of crisis or despair. Who would be that support if I struck out on my own? Who could get to me in a 10-minute drive if I needed them? Who would be my emergency contact? Hell, for that matter, what type of social life could I hope to have with no support network – no one to babysit? I lived five states away from the only family with whom I communicated other than Bob's. I didn't have any real friends to call my own and would most likely lose all of our shared friends to Bob in the divorce. I had coworkers whom I barely knew and an aging Yorkshire terrier. That's what I had. I was a mom working a 50+ hour-a-week corporate job. I was no longer in a band with people I had come to call friends, but rather was trying to form a new band with a bunch of guys in our basement that neither Bob nor I knew well. They were all but strangers to us at this point. I had virtually no savings and was not sure if my parents were able to help me if something came up even though they always had. Bob's family, while not rich but comfortable, supplied an added sense of security in this area should an emergency arise.

How could I do this? How could I consider this? How could I risk this most wonderful family? Yet, what choice did I really have? Could I continue going through life living on Bob's plan? What could I be if I had no one else to make my decisions for me? What experiences might I have if I took charge of my life? Oh, so many questions! I just couldn't leave them all unanswered. They would drive me insane. I had to figure it out on my own.

## *Divorcing the Extended Family*

So I made the announcement of our divorce, and Bob's entire family was there for him. Maybe they were there for me, too, but I didn't dare ask. Suddenly, I saw myself as an intruder on their family. I felt I had betrayed everyone's expectations. They were devastated by my decision and really didn't understand what was so awful about my life. But the truth is it wasn't awful. It was just unlived. And my life couldn't go like a Christmas package that never got opened. This was something I wasn't going to have much luck explaining to anyone – not Bob and certainly not his loving, almost-perfect family. I'm not even sure I understood it myself. But I couldn't just get over it!

Life after marriage felt at times more like a game show than it did a Christmas present I was finally opening. In the first round, behind door #1, was a group of new friends who would become my new surrogate family and bring joy to my life for years to come (and still do). In the second round, behind door #2, I discovered more failed romantic relationships and a couple of less-than-lucrative career moves.

I liken the early days of our separation to feeling like Bob's entire family had been killed in some horrific accident. I really thought it would just be too hard for them to remain in my life. I certainly wouldn't expect them to betray Bob for my sake. Didn't associating with me mean they would have to do just that? Or did it? Could Bob find it in his heart and everyone's best interest to give his family permission to allow a continued relationship with me? I don't know how those conversations might have went, but somehow, through all of the hurt and pain he found a way to show me this mercy. And so did they.

## *Putting it All Back Together*

After Bob and I separated, Sandy, Dick, and Debbie continued to include me in their lives. Sandy continues to this day to send me Christmas and birthday cards. We call each other occasionally just to catch up, and I try diligently to keep Bob's family apprised of significant events in Ian's life so they don't miss out on anything. When I was young, they babysat him when I needed them to. We share pictures. We attend family gatherings together. When any of Bob's family attended Ian's soccer games, school concerts, or other activities, I would always sit with them, and, in fact, save them seats. I felt no need or desire to separate myself from them. It seemed so much more natural to be with them. It wasn't me and them. It was us – Ian's family!

I've shared in the difficult times with Bob's family, too. When Bob's Aunt Angie was dying with liver failure, I stood in the hospital room with the family surrounding her as she took her last breath. When Sandy's sister and Dick's son each passed, I attended their viewings and shared in the family's grief. When Bob and Brandi needed a sitter for their daughter, I watched her for them. When Bob was in a motorcycle accident, I immediately offered whatever support was needed. When Ian's grandfather, Dick, was in his last moments, I joined the family in hospice, cried with them, and celebrated his life with them in the moments following his funeral as the family gathered. It's just what people who care about each other do. And why on Earth should I not care about my son's father, grandmother, grandfather, or aunt?

I'm very thankful that Bob's family has remained in my life and that I can still call them my family too!

Ian with Grandparents (Bob's mom and stepdad, and Teresa's In-laws), Sandy and Dick

## *A Son's Perspective*

I'm incredibly grateful for my family. While it may be one of the most confusing family trees anyone's ever seen, I love it. A family built around love and support is all anyone can ask for, and that's all I've ever known from both sides and all branches. Reading this chapter, I really just want to thank my dad and his side of the family for not making my mom feel alone. I can't imagine how hard and scary it would have been for her knowing her only blood relative within 1,000 miles was her five-year old son. "Props" to her and my dad for pushing through it all.

Sometimes, it really seems like they did the impossible. But this is not fiction. The story here is true, and the love is real, and the results are observable and amazing.

---

With family relationships stabilized, there was still the matter of friendships to contemplate. For all of those who had endured our awkward fights and mean words toward one another, would any survive our divorce? Again I reflected on how our friendship network had evolved. Our friends together all originated with Bob's interests in Harleys, softball teammates and their wives or girlfriends, and holdovers from his childhood. Would I be relegated to socializing with the other soccer moms at Ian's games and a new group of coworkers who didn't share my past? Hmm . . . maybe that was a good thing. Would all of our joint friends choose Bob and abandon me? Were endless awkward encounters my destiny? Or would I simply withdraw into a cocoon of books and cooking for one every other week? And so Teresa's friendship makeover took flight.

## *Chapter 8*
## *The Friendship Web: A Tangled Mess for Divorcees*

Friendships are the collateral damage of every divorce. For that matter, they were probably the collateral damage of your marriage. At least they were in our case.

I really do appreciate our friends who put up with us during our marriage as we fought over euchre, volleyball, and pretty much any competitive situation we found ourselves in. I think we even fought about fighting. When we were together, our friends would literally conspire to ensure we *didn't* end up on the same teams just to avoid having to put up with the incessant arguing that was sure to ensue. I'm sure some of you reading this right now are fondly reminiscing (NOT!) about those days. Yeah, you know who you are. Thanks for continuing to be our friends in spite of what we put you through!

When our marriage ended, I thought very carefully about how to proceed with friends. After all, it wasn't their problem to solve, and they shouldn't be inconvenienced because of our decisions. Or at least I owed it to them to minimize the conflict.

*Teresa Harlow*

There were those friends whom we came into the relationship with. Bob's friends. My friends. There were those with whom we developed friendships together. And then there were those friends acquired during the course of the marriage who only knew one of us. These were our coworkers and such with whom we only socialized absent the other spouse.

In my case, I came into my relationship with Bob bringing only a couple of friends with me while he, on the other hand, was part of a large group of friends from his childhood. In the nine years we were married, we hung out almost exclusively with his friends, their girlfriends or wives, and their friends. I became casual friends with some of the women. But mostly, I was Bob's wife – a friend-in-law. So when we divorced, they had no vested interest in me. Those friendships simply fell away, and I would go on to find new and lasting friendships.

There were also some mutual friends who meant the world to me even though they were part of Bob's scene, if you will. I gave a lot of distance to them, too, for quite a while, unable to figure out how to continue a friendship with them without it being awkward for everyone. Over time, once Bob and I developed a friendship beyond our divorce and could comfortably be seen as two separate people rather than The Bob and Teresa Show, we did again end up all together in the same place – me, Bob, and Bob's friends. Most memorable are my son's band performances. As I was the consummate promoter of all things "Ian," of course I wanted as many people to pack an event as we could muster. Whether I knew them or not. Whether they liked me or not. They were not there for me. They were there supporting our son. So if they were willing to forego any awkward feelings and show up, I was going to do my damnedest to thank them for coming and take a genuine interest in them being there.

## *Happily Divorced*

Of course, since Bob and I got together in the first place because we had a lot in common, including our tastes in music and social settings, we frequently found ourselves with our different groups of friends in the same venue. When this happened very early in the divorce, I sometimes relocated out of courtesy to our friends and a desire to avoid confrontation – particularly when Bob had arrived first and I was with Steve, not his favorite person. Eventually, it felt okay and even enjoyable to stay under these circumstances and to reconnect with some of the special people from Bob's life with whom I had lost touch. Today, when Bob and Brandi host parties at their house and I'm invited, it feels quite natural to freely interact with the group. We genuinely treat each other as friends, joke around, give compliments when warranted, and catch up on our lives just like any friends do.

The few with whom we both had a mutually strong bond was more difficult to manage at the onset of our divorce. First, there was our friend Paul, who was Bob's friend first but with whom I had worked on a couple music projects over the years. Upon learning of our divorce, Paul promptly declared to Bob that he was "with him." NICE! *That* one kind of hurt. But even so, when I run into him now, it's amicable and a pleasant stroll down memory lane.

Then there was our boating couple, Bill and Crystal. We went on vacations together, hung out at their house on the weekends quite frequently, and even lived with them for a couple months when our house was being built. This was a much more difficult relationship for either of us to lose. It was true that Bob and Bill were closer than I was with either Bill or Crystal. Still, I really didn't want to lose them altogether. So for the first few months after the divorce, we literally took turns hanging out with them on alternating weekends. Crystal used to joke that it was their weekend with me or Bob. I appreciated their friendship very much in those days while I began to derive friendships of my own making for the first time in my adult life. Crystal and Bill had also been in my son's life since his birth. So hanging out with them was another activity that provided continuity for Ian. Eventually, I backed away from them as I formed new friendships; although we still talk and laugh together when we end up in the same places.

Let's face it. Your friendships post-divorce are going to change. If you hung out with certain couples before your divorce, that isn't going to happen afterwards – at least not in the same way. You and your ex probably aren't going to double-date with a "friend couple" you had when you were together. And at least for a while, anyway, and maybe forever, you won't be showing up to the same parties with another date. Even if *you* would be fine with this, it will make everyone else uncomfortable for quite a while. So don't do it for at least maybe a year. It's really asking too much of your friends and your ex. Unless you relish situations that are volatile and you enjoy provoking confrontation, I would not go there.

There are also those couples who will fear that your divorce may be contagious. If they hang out with you, they may soon find themselves in divorce court. These are normally the ones who are less than secure in their own marriages or possibly have moral problems with divorce altogether. These couples will make up every excuse in the book to avoid you or will simply stop answering your calls. Don't sweat it. Give them time. Eventually, they may decide they value the friendship with one or both of you and invite you back into their lives. If they don't, simply move on.

If you are both single for a while after your divorce and you plan to head to the party of a mutual friend, it's going to be very awkward for a while. It may be best to avoid this situation to give everyone time to adjust to seeing the two of you without one another first. Then, maybe show up with someone else only if you are absolutely certain the other isn't going to be there. Look, it's called respect for other's feelings. Always think about how you would want to be considered and treated. This will normally keep you from drifting into turbulent waters. Bear in mind your friends may be grieving the loss of their couple-friend, too. Or, they may be relieved to not have to withstand your arguing with one another in front of them anymore. I'm sure we left plenty of people feeling that way. Either way, they don't need you thrusting more negative energy into their lives.

If you are on your own divorce journey, try to remember it is not all about you. Practice the Golden Rule. You may very well find yourself one day right in the middle of the bridge you considered burning.

---

The evolution of friendships is not confined to those outside your marriage. If you were lucky enough to share a friendship with your former spouse, there is a chance that will survive the divorce as well. You can at least give it a fighting chance. Just because you don't live under the same roof anymore doesn't have to mean you can't enjoy talking to each other about the stuff that typical friends share. Tread lightly and with compassion. But don't close off the idea that your friendship can continue in a different light. As Bob and I became separate single people, we found ourselves talking about matters dealing with Ian pretty regularly and comfortably. And since we were friends when we started our relationship, it wasn't too far-fetched for us to want to share stories about our evolving singleness as well. In the next chapter, I talk about how this progression worked for us.

## *Chapter 9*
## *Single Life: Weird Conversations with the Ex*

Some of the weirdest conversations Bob and I have had as a divorced couple revolved around our adventures as single people – not because the experiences were particularly weird but because it is just odd to talk to someone you used to be intimate with about someone whom they may be picturing you someday being intimate with. It's probably hard for a lot of you to understand how we could discuss our evolving single-ness. It might even be making you a little squirmy right now. Like where the hell is this going? No worries. It's really not creepy. At least not to me.

Perhaps it will make more sense to you if you consider that neither Bob nor I had spent any real time as adult singles before the point at which we divorced from each other. When we divorced, we were both mid-30s and single for the first times in our adult lives. Bob had begun dating a woman right out of high school whom he eventually married and then divorced within a year. I had pretty much paralleled this pattern. I met a guy two weeks before my high school senior prom and proceeded to date him for three and half years. I eventually married him when I was 21 and promptly separated from him six months later. About 8 months after that, I met Bob.

*Teresa Harlow*

So I guess for us, our union developed rather prematurely, before we were done experiencing single life. Once the shock and sadness of our failed marriage had run a reasonable course and we had committed ourselves to remain friends, it was sort of natural for us to share about our single-life escapades. I think this was mostly helpful since it allowed our friendship to continue to evolve to a natural state of post-marital bliss and remove all the awkward overtones of sexual jealousy and disappointment that I think other couples harbor against one another long after the possibility of ever having sex again with each other has evaporated. It also helped us to truly learn from our experiences together. Basically, if you are sharing as friends do about relationships with others of the opposite sex, it becomes natural to offer opinions on what might work or not work. It also offers a weirdly safe audience since no one knows your dating habits and style better than one who actually experienced it.

These conversations weren't possible in the early days of our separation or divorce. But Bob and I both accepted the fact we were happier not cohabiting pretty quickly. After about a year, we began to cheer for the happily-ever-after ending that we each felt the other truly deserved in spite of our failure with one another.

Believe me, I didn't approve of all of Bob's dating choices, and he downright opposed at least my first choice – the man who I met the weekend before I announced my intention to separate from him. I have to say, given this circumstance, Bob put forth an amazing effort to be cordial to Steve for the three years we dated. Thinking back on it, I really don't know if I could have done the same. But I truly do thank Bob for doing this in spite of the pain he must have felt every time he had to look at the man he considered the "other guy." By the time I had moved on from this first new someone, Bob had remarried and seemed to want me to find someone, too. We even got to a point where Brandi, his new wife, and I talked about my dating situations--not in vivid detail mind you—but on a more general "found anyone special?" level.

To clarify, sharing your dating experiences with your ex isn't advisable for everyone. And you certainly should not do it if it is even a remote possibility that it may inflict pain on the former spouse. That will only do harm to your efforts as a happily divorced couple. In my case, I didn't consider sharing these types of things with my ex until he did it first, which assumes I was in a position to handle it. I was. So it worked out.

If you are on the receiving end of this scenario – your ex is sharing his or her dating experiences with you – try not to assume it's an attempt to hurt you, but rather may be an effort to normalize your relationship as friends and remove the awkwardness. Look, the fact is you're not likely going back there. Some people do this. But I guess what I'm saying is if it is over for the two of you, why not move on to a place of comfortable non-awkward friendship, which includes sharing our successes and failures in dating. And if you're lucky enough to have an ex-spouse who is as funny as Bob when telling a story, you might even derive a bit of entertainment out of it.

---

A failed marriage can really do a number on your ability to think objectively and rationally about new potential mates. Maybe you've spent years in a passionless relationship. You look around and all you see are happy couples holding hands, gazing into each other's eyes, and declaring their undying love for one another. You admire their joy, their happiness, and their acceptance of one another and wonder, "Am I even capable of that?" If others can be happy, why can't I? Then someone – a complete stranger – looks at you with soft eyes. He laughs at your stupid jokes and tells you that you really are perfect. And suddenly you are driven by desire to dive headlong back into the deep waters of romance. But it's so soon. Is it too soon? Ah, what the heck – I've been unhappy long enough. Let's go!

## *Chapter 10*
## *Rebounders: A Cautionary Tale*

For many of us who have lost that loving feeling in our previous relationships, something pretty strange can happen when we divorce. Suddenly uncoupled, we acquire a voracious appetite for that over-the-top love affair we see in the movies. We tell ourselves, "Sure, I failed in my last relationship, but I can still be swept off my feet. I can still have my happily ever after! In fact, I long for it. I must have it, and I must have it now!"

So we become open, maybe too open, to new possibilities before we've really worked through our failings, taken inventory of our lessons, and given serious thought to what we want in a future relationship. Before we know it, someone shows us affection, respect, and tells us how beautiful we are, and all at once, our rational-self forgets to go into a new relationship eyes wide open. We plunge head-first into the deep end and are completely consumed not by the other person's *actual* wonder but rather by the *idea* of the perfect relationship. We discount any shortcomings we witness in the new interest and find it effortless to only focus on the immense feelings provoked when in the presence of this new someone. We feel sexy again. Our hearts race with excitement. Colors seem brighter. The sun shines and warms our hearts. We dance like kids again with complete reckless abandon. Just thinking about this new relationship is exhilarating.

But if only we paused, we'd realize that we're not actually thinking about the new love interest so much as we are thinking about the *feelings* of love, lust, and excitement that this new relationship stirs in us. If someone, a friend, dares to impose on the perfect imagery we've created around this new person, we dismiss it – that is, if we ever even hear it in the first place. Oh, our friends just don't understand. They don't remember what this feels like. And they can't know what they're talking about. He's perfect. We're perfect! So we pour our hearts and souls into these new relationships losing ourselves and our perspective entirely. One, or many in some cases, might even say we've lost our minds!

Yes, new love is a great thing – an enthralling experience. Really, there isn't much else like it. I can think of few other events throughout our lives that provoke such intense positive emotion. But this intensity can also be blinding, and in many cases, short-lived. Further, it may deny us the opportunity to learn to love and honor ourselves. Then one day, sort of like that moment when we reach the bottom of the first hill of a roller coaster, the lust ends, our eyes flutter open, and we're not sure if we like this ride after all. We feel a bit nauseous, and through the fog, we can't even figure out how we got here or how this person that seemed so perfect at first is suddenly revealing a side that we hadn't even noticed was there all the time. This isn't necessarily because the new love isn't a good person. He or she may have lots of redeeming qualities but just may not have those qualities that will sustain the two into their elder years. We may find this person is worthy to reside in our lives for a chapter or two but not an entire novel. Surprised, shocked, and deeply saddened, we realize we just read the last page of our book together.

These experiences can certainly run the gamut. Once we actually snap out of our dream state, we begin to notice annoying habits we just can't come to terms with. Maybe the other person doesn't share our values. Maybe he or she isn't even as attractive as we once thought. Where did that beer gut come from anyway? Cupid be damned, I tell you! In extreme cases, one may find out the person has a criminal record or becomes abusive. I was fortunate to escape these extreme circumstances. But not everyone is.

Why am I telling you all this? It isn't to scare you or to suggest that you can't find the perfect love again. It's just to raise some awareness that with that first relationship after marriage, you may be giving it more credit than it is due. So consumed by the idea of love and to prove you don't suck as a partner, you could actually miss the fact that you aren't really experiencing love at all but rather heightened human hormones, a.k.a. lust – an unsustainable illusion. Now there's nothing wrong with lust, either. But I would suggest that lust in the absence of real love can actually be dangerous because of how it manipulates our otherwise logical deduction processes. And I really believe we are more susceptible to this in that first relationship following a long-term failed one than after having a series of "learning relationships." These are the ones that provide us a feedback loop within which we *consciously decide* what we like and don't like to experience. We learn what type of conversations and experiences we enjoy having with another person. We learn what type of lifestyle we really want to create for ourselves – what friend circle really serves us. In short, we learn more about ourselves. If we're really lucky, we might even learn to honor ourselves and insist on our own happiness first.

So as you become your *new* self, just be cautious of that first relationship that catapults you into the heavens. Be mindful not to bury your head in the sand. Don't abandon your rational thinking. And if you do have a rebound relationship that ends, don't be surprised if it hurts even worse than the divorce. A bubble that bursts is usually more startling than a ball that slowly deflates.

---

Once you have entered into a new romantic relationship, you'll inevitably have to consider if and when you should introduce the new person to the ex. Ideally, there will be a reasonable gap of time between your divorce and the encounter with the new someone – something I did not achieve. Or you may be wondering when you'll have to face seeing your ex with another man or woman. Maybe the thought alone makes you feel sick to your stomach. In the next chapter, I share the introduction of Bob to my first serious relationship partner, Steve, and how each of us managed both the planned and unplanned encounters.

## *Chapter 11*
## *Meeting the Ex's New Someone: Do I Have to?*

The experience of introducing a new someone to the ex-spouse or having your ex introduce his or her new love interest to you will probably feel a lot like a rerun from the moment one of you asked for a divorce. It's as if a stake is being driven through the heart of a once-promising relationship . . . ensuring it will never be brought back to life. When a child is involved, it introduces an entirely new set of considerations. In Chapter 12, I'll focus on the introductions to the children. But first, in this chapter, we need to address the elephant in the room. Do you see her? It's the new girlfriend.

Depending on how much you and your ex-spouse cared about each other, one or both of you could be mortified by the thought of the other being with someone else. Anyone else! So while *you* may have decided it's time to introduce the new boyfriend or girlfriend to everyone, you may want to consider how this information will be received by the *ex*. For the best chance of preserving a caring relationship with the other parent, remember to be kind and **honor the Golden Rule** when doing this. It will serve you both better as you continue to interact as co-parents.

*Teresa Harlow*

Looking back, I wasn't as kind as I would have liked someone to be to me in those early days. Sure, I waited about six months before introducing my son to the new guy in my life. But on the other hand, I interjected the concept of another man into the relationship as part of the separation announcement to Bob. The proverbial "there's someone else," I believe, were my words. I was operating under the false pretense that this somehow softened the blow to Bob and gave me license in his eyes to do what I was doing. After all, would it be fair to anyone for our relationship to continue if my heart weren't in it? I told myself over and over again that this was best for everyone since I couldn't remain committed to Bob. It would hurt at first, but eventually, he would end up in a relationship in which he and the other person were better matched. He would find the love he deserved. *I* was convinced based on one weekend that I had found someone who I could go on to love and grow old with.

Ok, we didn't grow old together. As I mentioned, I dated that first guy after *us* for three and a half years, and we had some really good times. But we eventually parted. Today, after an excruciating and very long search for Mr. Right, I can finally say I have found that special, lasting love in my current fiancé, Brian. Bob went on to meet Brandi, whom he now considers the love of his life. They have built a wonderful life together, and I am so happy for them.

Of course I skipped over how the introduction of my first new relationship went. So I'll share that here, and you can decide for yourself whether or not I handled this well. I certainly wasn't perfect, but I did always try to keep the thought of kindness to Bob in my heart and sought to minimize negatives it might bring to our ongoing relationship as co-parents. In the end, I guess I was successful. Or probably more aptly put, we – Bob and I – were successful since we *are* still friends.

Further, I think our son respects the choices each of us has made along the way and has certainly been witness to this kind treatment to one another.

As previously mentioned, I told Bob from the beginning that there was someone else. From what I recall, he had limited interactions with the "new guy" early on, at least. We'd sometimes end up at the same local bar playing pool or watching a band – both activities Bob and I were doing when we first met. In these situations, I think I was truly more gracious toward Bob than my date was. He didn't really let me see it, but I got the distinct impression that probably like most men, he gave the look and moved with me in my space in a way that sent the painful message to Bob that he had lost me and someone else now had me.

Fortunately for Bob, I didn't really have too many close friends I carried forward after our separation. So our unplanned run-ins were fairly infrequent occurrences. Of course, after the boyfriend met Ian, I invited him to accompany me to Ian's soccer games. Knowing Bob was uncomfortable with him and sensing that the boyfriend might even seek to provoke him, I minimized their encounters and those activities I invited the boyfriend to attend with me. Still, Bob remained cordial when he was there and even on occasion made it a point to speak to this guy, whom he could not stand. I introduced Bob to the man's daughter at one of Ian's soccer games. When he later encountered her at my house, Bob was always very nice to her, being the usual funny guy just like he would be with anyone else. He did such a great job of separating any emotions he had about our relationship from the innocent kids in the scenario. I am very grateful to him for that.

---

Introducing Bob to Steve was hard. But how on earth was I going to introduce my son to the new guy? Good Lord! Will life ever feel normal again? Maybe this is the new normal. A life filled with awkward moment after awkward moment.

## Chapter 12
## Shaky Ground: Bringing New Adults into Our Child's Life

How long should you date someone before he or she meets your child? How do you explain this new "someone" to your child? What if your child doesn't like the new person? What if the new person doesn't like your child? Okay, actually, that last one is easy: Dump 'em like a hot potato! What if your child just needs to give the new person a chance? What if your *child* loves the new person but *you* stop liking them? What if the new someone has kids? A crazy ex? Smelly animals? A dirty house? Weird idiosyncrasies? A criminal background? Alright, again, this last one is pretty easy for me: You're outta here, Jack! And I haven't even touched on the possibility – or in many cases, likelihood – that the ex will hate the new guy and make your life a living hell. After considering all the ways this could go badly, maybe it is just best to bail on the whole idea and to vow celibacy until your kids are grown. It's only 12 or so years away, right?

Of course, some people do make this sacrifice. But while it is the best path for some, I considered what my child could gain from a new relationship in his life. Not a new dad, but just a new someone, whatever that someone would come to mean to him. In my case at least, Ian already had a great dad. So we didn't need to replace him. I did, however, think it would be a great thing for Ian to witness a better example of two people lovingly interacting with one another – something that, unfortunately, he did not witness between Bob and me in his early years.

One of the most threatening aspects of getting divorced is the prospect that some other woman might someday claim parental rights – even mommy rights – over our children. For me, being a mom was and still is the most important contribution I will ever make to this world. How could I bear the thought of that being taken from me? I agonized over this possibility as Bob began to embark on new relationships. At the time, it didn't even occur to me that Bob was facing this fear already from a dad's perspective. As I went straight from our marriage into another relationship, Bob had to deal with that right away *while* simultaneously grieving the end of our marriage. Wow! This stuff is really painful to remember.

Even now, I feel Bob's pain in the pit of my stomach. And I re-live the anxiety I felt over the mere thought of another woman interacting with my child in a mommy-like capacity. Twenty years removed from these events, I can now more fully appreciate how Bob conducted himself toward me in those early days in spite of some of my less-than-ideal choices.

I think it was about five months before Bob began dating again. The first lady that he saw regularly seemed to care for him *and* Ian for that matter. But she could have been Mother Teresa and I would have still feared her. I couldn't shake a nagging feeling that she was going to become the "stepmom" and then turn into some evil bitch from hell one day. The thought that this might happen in front of my only son terrified me. On the other hand, what if Ian liked her and then Bob ended it? Ian would be hurt. What if she was careless? Could Ian get hurt in her care? After all, she was not a mom. What if she physically or mentally abused my son? Of course I expected that Bob was careful about who he exposed our son to, just as I was. But the fact is many of us know at least one person who was abused in some way by a stepparent, boyfriend, or girlfriend of a parent. If that were to happen, it would be all she wrote for me. I'd have to kill her. Then I'd go to prison and my life would be over.

Thankfully, Bob was careful about introducing women to Ian. He dated the first woman for a bit, and I went to therapy to get control over my anxiety. The best piece of advice I ever got from my therapist was worth every dollar: She reminded me that if I believed Bob was a good dad, I'd just have to trust him. I had to accept his choices and put my trust in knowing he would continue to be a good father. Fortunately, in my case, I really did believe, above all else, that Bob would protect our son from any harm – either physical or mental. He had grown up in a situation where a stepmom had been pretty nasty toward him. So I had confidence Bob would not let the same treatment happen to his son. And with that, I released my fears about that first woman and those that followed. I really did want Bob to be happy, whatever that meant for him, as long as it also made my son happy. Look, I'm a mom. I can't help it. I will always want to protect him.

On my side of the equation, I decided on a minimum six-month dating rule before I would introduce anyone to Ian. This, I felt, would be safer and more considerate to him *and* the other person. There would be no constant parade of potential stepparents and no mixed signals sent to the potential mate, either. Ian would see that I was being selective and would be assured that I would always protect him. I also didn't want to disappoint him. Above all else, though, I wanted to find out more about someone before putting our son at risk.

After six months of dating Steve, I decided it was time Ian met him. Steve had a daughter a couple years older than Ian. She and I met fairly soon after we started dating. That was her father's choice, and given his odd situation with the daughter's mom, I can somewhat understand why he made this choice. The couple had an excessively tumultuous relationship with ongoing restraining orders, that ridiculous nine-year long custody battle, the mom frequently withholding visitation, and one instance in which she fled the state illegally with the child moving the two of them to Maryland. The father had to hire a private investigator to track them down and force her to return with the daughter to Ohio. What a mess! So dad had been through a lot to remain in his daughter's life, and I think he really just wanted her to see a man and woman together who were not fighting. I got along well with the daughter, and she seemed to enjoy my company.

## *The Introduction*

When it was time everyone met – the daughter and Ian, Ian and the boyfriend--Ian was only six years old. So I didn't want to make this some big life-changing event – at least not in his young mind. I just wanted all of us to get together and have a nice time. I figured Ian and the daughter might play and get to know each other and Ian might at least become semi-comfortable with the presence of another man around me. So I planned a gathering of my new post-divorce friend group to play cards and invited the boyfriend and his daughter to join us. I asked everyone to make it seem like nothing more than a bunch of friends getting together at mom's house with a chance for Ian to meet a new playmate.

*Happily Divorced*

Everyone arrived around seven or so, and we had a lovely time playing cards while the kids played. And played. And played. In fact, it seemed these two were long-lost relatives. They really were like immediate best friends. All my friends noticed and commented on how natural they seemed to be together and how much fun they were having – entirely oblivious to the existence of anyone else. Finally, the friends left, and it was just the four of us. Steve and I watched a movie on the couch in the living room while the kids continued to play in the next room. The kids had the time of their lives playing with action figures together and giggling their heads off. The night was a success and a relief. Now we could all spend time together without fear that someone was going to hate someone else.

Meanwhile, Bob dated a few women here and there, and then after about 2 years, he met a new redhead. Her name was Brandi. She was a little younger than us—not absurdly so, but just young enough to tease Bob about it a little. But more importantly, she had substance. I could tell she cared deeply for Bob and had patience for some of his antics that I simply lacked. She also had an obvious maternal instinct of her own and clicked well with Ian. I'm so glad that Bob kept looking until he found Brandi. We are all better off with her in our family's corner.

---

New home, new relationship, new friends. We're all set, right? Ready to take on anything. Now how does a divorced person with a single child and no relatives in state celebrate the holidays, anyway? Does the child spend this time with mom or dad? What about traveling to those long-distance relatives? Of course if you do that, then the other parent misses out and the child does without him or her over the holidays. Then again, play it fair and *you* miss out on special moments with your child. Crap! I hadn't really thought about any of this.

## Chapter 13
## Happy Holidays: Are They Still Possible?

Holidays – a time for joy, fun, and celebration – are a challenging time of year for any family. Everyone talks grandly about family, particularly during the holidays. Beautiful holiday dinners, hours spent decorating together, shopping for gifts, and laughing jubilantly as they play family games with extended family. Yeah, we all know the truth. Many family traditions play out more like a scene from *Christmas Vacation* fraught with dysfunction of all types. Fights between relatives, catty exchanges among the women, and the men constantly working to one-up each other's manliness whether that's through material success or who can belch the loudest, if that is their calling.

For divorced people with children, the holidays serve up the added challenges of dividing time with the children between two parents, grandparents, and other extended family members and facing the devastation of missing out on precious memories with your child. As parents, isn't it our duty to create family traditions? Yet that is very difficult to do when you've agreed to alternate holidays. At best, your tradition is either only executed in alternating years, or you carry it out on a different day from year to year. While this may work fine for you and your child or children, it is hard to pull off when considering the broader family. Grandma and Grandpa may always host Thanksgiving at their house. A particular holiday tradition may only take place on Christmas Eve each year. We all hope to establish lasting traditions with our children that we can enjoy together for decades and that they can take forward with them throughout their lives.

It gets exponentially more complicated when there are multiple divorces, remarriages, stepchildren, and even pets that have to be worked into the equation. So my best advice is to not get too caught up in your own feelings. This will just drive you crazy, and honestly, it isn't just about YOU! Hell, this is the case even if you're not divorced.

In our family, not only were Bob and I divorced. Bob's parents were divorced – and both remarried. Bob eventually got remarried, and his wife's mom got remarried. Bob's sister was married, but her husband's family lived two hours away. My parents were still married but lived in Texas, 1,500 miles away. In fact, none of my relatives lived in town. This actually ended up being a bit of a Godsend. Oh, it was tough not having them close by, and I hated that we couldn't share more of our lives with them. But had they, too, been local, it would have just been one more difficult choice to have to make when it came to dividing up our time.

When you are divorced with kids, the holidays are simply a minefield of anxiety. How do you get it right? How do you build traditions when you constantly have to consider the forces outside of your home? How do you balance what your child wants with what you want to experience as a parent? I can only speak for myself. But I didn't work on getting pregnant for two years only to miss all the significant memories in my son's life. My dreams of building that vast photo album of costumes and pictures with Santa didn't end with my divorce. I know there are people who let these things go. But honestly, I just don't relate to this type of parenting existence. I couldn't let Bob's prophecy of "You're going to miss half of his life" come to fruition.

So not unlike the tangled web we had to weave to establish our living arrangements, we once again had to exhibit selflessness, flexibility, and compassion to provide the best holiday experiences to our boy while still getting to enjoy being his parents.

One other thing I would caution against in the case of holidays is giving the kids TOO MUCH control in deciding how their holiday time is spent. It isn't all about them, either! Certainly strive to make it fair and not too frantic to enjoy. But seriously, burdening a child with the decision of who to spend time with and how much and who to pick between is more unfair. Make it your burden to figure out. Not theirs. Be the adults. Be fair to yourself, too. Being a martyr doesn't serve your or your children's interests. After all, they want to spend time with you.

Ian as Robin, Age 2

## *Halloween*

The first key to a Happy Halloween whether you are divorced or still married is to let your child pick his or her own costume. It's one of the few things they can control. So let them have it. Pick one costume that they will want to wear to both parents' house. That way, there is one experience – not only for them but for the two parents and everyone else around them as well! Remember, the grandparents are building a photo album as well.

Now, you might be saying to yourself, "Well, of course you let the kid pick their costume. What crazy control freak would deny a child such a rite of passage?" But I can tell you from another divorced couple I know that this is not the case. In the ongoing obsession to control every aspect of every experience her children have, this mother picks what the kids wear. The outcome is that once the kids are out of her sight, they strip down the costume to the point that you can't even tell what they are dressed as.

Beyond the costume, I'd say the more tricky part (pardon the pun) for us was how to deal with the logistics of trick-or-treat. And in our case, we lived very close, which made it a little easier. Still, will the kids go to both neighborhoods? Will they just do one? Is there time for both? Will they have anyone to go with in both neighborhoods at different times? What do *they* want to do? What if I don't get to see my child in his costume this year? Oh, hell! This part sucks. Looking back, I guess we did "ok" with this one, but I think we could have done better.

Ian did pick his costumes and also which neighborhood to start in. But the other parent always wanted to be part of it, and so Ian would have to stop halfway through the first neighborhood to switch houses. Of course, he didn't get to go with the other kids in the second neighborhood because they had started way earlier and were either done or on an entirely different part of the neighborhood. I think in some years he picked one or the other neighborhood but still had to make time to share his costume with each parent. As parents and the adults, we should have made all this inconvenience more our affair and let him just enjoy the experience in one location or the other. Being the true Libra sun sign that he is, Ian probably felt obligated to give each parent and friend-group equal time, anyway. So I'm not sure that he would have chosen any differently. But looking back, I feel we should have done more to relieve him of this burden.

So as you finalize your plans for this year's trick-or-treating, do everything you can to remember this is a memory for your child first, and you second. Be flexible and considerate. And expect to do more than your friends who are married have to just to create the same level of kid-parent experience.

## *Thanksgiving*

*Our blended family – Parker, Madison, Ian, Teresa, and Brian (taking photo) - holiday meal*

Enjoying Thanksgiving has probably been the biggest challenge for me. When Ian was between six and fourteen years old, since none of my family lived close, I mostly conceded Thanksgiving to Bob and his family. It was just too sad for me to make dinner for just Ian and me. Plus it didn't seem right to keep him from enjoying a big family gathering that Bob could provide. Nor did it feel right to cart Ian off with me to Texas and have he and his dad and denied their experience. So I would do something else. I'd have probably been better off in these years before Brian had I went to volunteer at a homeless shelter or elderly home. I don't know why I didn't do that other than to say I think I just got caught up wallowing in my own despair. Instead, I usually met up at a bar on Thanksgiving evening with friends trying to escape the family scene.

I remember once Ian called me and asked me, "How can a son not see his mom on Thanksgiving?" Possibly the saddest question a child could ever ask a parent. It was just awful. Yep, there was that half of Ian's life Bob said I'd miss. It's in my eardrum right now thrashing at my heart. Seriously, what a waste all that self-pity was! If you end up alone on the holidays, don't do what I did. Do something that involves you giving your time and energy to someone else's needs. I think you'll feel a whole lot better.

When I finally started seeing Brian seriously, we began alternating Thanksgivings. Of course, this introduced more complications – Brian's kids, their mom's wishes, her new husband, and her parents' schedule. Ian is now 25, and we still haven't really mastered Thanksgiving. Given that I consider Thanksgiving the quintessential family holiday, it just comes preloaded with anxiety year after year. Still, alternating seems like the kindest choice for all involved.

## *Christmas*

Christmas – it's supposed to be a season of good tidings. In reality, it is a full-on stress-fest! Working parents, single parents, and remarried parents strive to create a greeting-card-worthy experience for their children to remember throughout their lives. It's a LOT of pressure for anyone. But cut the hours and energy you have left to devote to this endeavor tremendously, and by December 23, many of us are entirely depleted of joy and just need to sleep.

*Happily Divorced*

For us in the early days of our divorce, when it came to Christmas, Ian was still young and into the whole Santa experience. These experiences, as we all know, are fleeting. As Christmas is this magical time for children, I really didn't want the first holiday memories Ian had of life post-Mr. and Mrs. Harlow to be of sadness. Nor did I want to bear the guilt of denying his father the experience of waking up where his son was on Christmas morning to find what Santa had left. So that first Christmas after our separation, I offered to let Bob stay in a guest room at my new house. It worked out great. Ian's Christmas was saved, and I would not die of guilt for denying Bob the joy of seeing his son's face light up at the sight of a magical Christmas morning.

The following year, Bob was still single and I was again on hiatus from Steve. So Bob invited me to stay at his house on the couch and to join them when the rest of the family – Bob's mom and step-dad, sister and her husband – came over to open gifts and have a family meal. Bob's mom even invited me to join them for Christmas Eve one year. We had a blast that night playing games together as a family with our son. As the years went by, Bob continued to include me in many family gatherings, and I included him in the few we hosted as well. This worked for us because at the core of it all, we still enjoyed each other's company. It may not work this smoothly for everyone. But don't

*Ian scores a 'Monster' ornament for Christmas*

assume it won't work. At the very least, be creative and look for opportunities that allow your child or children to enjoy time with everyone during the holidays without feeling the burden of choosing who to spend time with or feeling like they are spending all of their time being shuffled around from place to place.

Now that Ian is older, we are once again at a transition. It now falls to him to choose how he will spend his time. But at least his dad and I can be in the same place together and add, rather than detract, from the enjoyment of everyone around us. What an improvement over our marriage!

---

Besides Halloween, Thanksgiving, and Christmas, there are other special holidays which we needed to decide how to handle as a divorced couple with a child. Read on to learn how we handled birthdays and Mother's and Father's Day.

# Chapter 14
# Birthdays: Shared Celebrations

When it came to celebrating Ian's birthday, Bob and I traded off on this responsibility just like any other. One year I planned and paid for the kid party, and the next year Bob did. And when the special birthdays came up, we joined forces. This would sometimes mean going in on a nice gift together that we agreed on. And sometimes it meant we would have a party at one of our houses and invite the other parent and their family to attend. For me, this consisted of close friends and Brian's family. We each welcomed the other and their family into our home as we would any other friend, again able to put aside our otherwise competitive nature.

Ian's 18$^{th}$ Birthday celebration was held at Teresa's house with family from all sides in attendance. Pictured are Bob, Teresa, Ian, Brandi, and Gracie.

*Teresa Harlow*

On Ian's 18th birthday, we decided to play a little practical joke on him. Bob and I worked together to pack Ian's car with tons of balloons. Then we took turns writing funny sayings in washable car ink all over his car. Really, we had entirely too much fun with the whole thing. And when Ian saw the sayings, there was no doubt in his mind who wrote what as we both have our own unique flavor of humor. There really is nothing more fun than two parents teaming up to mildly embarrass their teenage son . . . in an innocent, no-harm-done sort of way, of course.

When it came to our birthdays, we also honored each other and kept things on positive footing by taking Ian to shop for gifts for each other and by giving him the money to pay for them without hesitation. This may sound easy enough. But I don't think it is all that normal among divorced couples. In fact, none of the other divorced people I knew either bought for the other parent or had gifts bought for them. I guess they just couldn't get past themselves. But for me, it was important for Ian to have the opportunity to buy his dad a gift of his choosing and get to see the joy on his face when he opened it. I couldn't take that from Ian. It wasn't my place. And I always tried not to let our divorce dictate how my son interacted with his father. If we had stayed married, I would have expected Ian to want to give his father a gift. So in divorce, this expectation was no different.

*Happily Divorced*

Another thing that we always made sure was possible was for Ian to spend the day with either Bob or I on our respective birthdays. Again, this seems obvious and logical, doesn't it? But surprisingly, I've seen way too many parents who don't even consider extending this simple courtesy – either planning a vacation or other activity that inhibits the child from celebrating the parents' birthdays. There is simply no excuse for this childish and thoughtless behavior as far as I'm concerned. For me, it is also important that the child learn to honor their parents' special days. It is important they learn to not only receive but to give. They had best learn that now so as not to be devastated by disappointment later. Or worse yet, grow up not knowing how to be generous and giving of themselves to others.

We did the same for each other on Mother's Day and Father's Day. I didn't even consider scheduling something that would interfere with Ian spending time with his dad on Father's Day, and I received the same treatment in return.

If you've read my chapter on Practicing the Golden Rule, this is what I'm talking about. If you always keep in mind how you would want to be treated, you will not stray from appropriate choices in matters of co-parenting. Remember, you get what you give. It is the universal law!

---

Some people look with dread toward attending their child's extracurricular activities because it will mean facing the ex-spouse and maybe the ex's extended family. But passing on these experiences robs the child of the opportunity to have a parent cheer for (or console) him or her, and capture their childhood in photos. In the next chapter, read how finding a way to coexist in these circumstances not only improved our son's experience, but also gave Bob and I an opportunity to strengthen our co-parenting relationship.

## *Chapter 15*
## *Soccer Mom (and Dad): Don't Miss Out!*

Parents of most elementary-age kids want to give their child the opportunity to try lots of different things so they can figure out what they like and discover their talents. Of course, every time one of these activities is added, it's another situation divorced parents must face where they will inevitably be in the same place together lest they miss out on the whole experience that their child has. So what do you do? Do you figure out an alternating schedule? Do you just not go and disappoint your child by not being there? And don't forget, it's not just the ex you'll have to face but probably other family members, and maybe a girlfriend or new spouse. Need this be another trip down Misery Lane?

Absolutely not! How about you just go and enjoy watching your child do his or her thing? I personally never considered any other option, and I don't think Bob did either. We both went. Of course, we did more than this to enhance the overall experience for ourselves, our son, and all those around us. We usually sat together and marveled in our son's greatness. Oh, stop it! We all do that! But look, in this case, it's a valuable bridge between your child's other parent and you. It's something you are likely to have in common – maybe the only thing once you're divorced. So consider this an advantage you can use to enhance the situation. You will actually enjoy the experience more by exchanging thoughts about your shared admiration as you revel in your child's efforts.

Okay, I have to admit, you will also be faced with some other possibilities. Like maybe your child won't be great at something. Maybe he will struggle. Maybe he will not enjoy a particular activity. Maybe there will be nothing marvelous about what the two of you witness together. Guess what? This too is a positive. What do I mean by that? Well, you will both witness it for yourself and not have to rely on the opinion of the other or just be left in the dark, unaware of your child's struggles. You may also talk about it together to form a unified strategy for addressing the situation whether that is to provide opportunities for improvement, allowing your child to bow out of a given activity, or consoling her when she faces disappointment. It is always better to be fully armed with the truth, and it is usually better to put two heads together to address a problem. Again, you have common ground. You want your child to be happy.

Ian played baseball for a few years and then focused his attention on soccer through the end of middle school. During that time, Bob and I went to the games and usually sat together. When he remarried, Brandi went to most games and we'd all sit together. When I became serious with Brian, he attended the games and we all sat together. On many occasions, Bob's mom and stepdad, sister and her husband, Ian's cousins, and Bob's dad and stepmom attended games. Each time, without hesitation or trepidation, we sat together and drank in the moments of Ian's childhood together. Who knew this is what they really meant by "for better or worse?"

I believe this experience served not only our purpose but also provided a great example to others of a choice they, too, could make. On several occasions throughout the years, I was told by other parents that they thought it was great how Bob and I got along and sat at the games together and enjoyed each other's company. Not only did they appreciate the fact they weren't dealt an awkward situation, but they weren't forced to choose between us either. They could freely communicate with both of us without some weird aura.

Now, we did a really good job, but we weren't perfect. There was a year – I think it might have been $4^{th}$ grade spring season – when Ian complained incessantly about going to practice. Every time we'd get ready to head to practice, it was a battle. "I like playing games. I don't like practice," He would say. I told him time and again, "This is part of the deal. You made a commitment and if you want to play the games, you have to go to practice." Finally, exasperated after having this fight repeatedly over the course of almost an entire season, I told Ian he wouldn't be playing the next year if he continued to complain. He dug in his heels and complained anyway, and I announced to him as the season was coming to a close that I had every intention of following through on my threat. There was no way I was going to sacrifice precious time dragging him unwillingly to practice for a game he enjoyed playing. So I had made up my mind that I wasn't going to sign him up next season. He didn't complain. He seemed to accept his plight.

Flash forward a few months until fall signups rolled around, and Bob informed me that he had signed Ian up for soccer. I told him that I had not intended to have Ian signed up this season. I guess I had failed to communicate this. He said it was already done and paid for. At first, I was angry that I wasn't going to be able to follow through since I am careful to always do so with Ian. Given the reality of this particular scenario and the fact I knew Ian really did like playing soccer and being part of the team, I decided to pivot rather than make more of it. After all, he did ask his dad to sign him up.

To make sure we didn't have a replay of the previous year, however, I decided to make sure Ian understood that he was getting one final reprieve on this. I told him in no uncertain terms, "Your dad signed you up for soccer this season because he was not aware of our deal. So here's how this is going to work. You get one more chance at this. Complain one time about going to practice and you will be done with soccer immediately. I will take you home and neither your father nor I will take you again. You'll be done with soccer. So make your choice. If you want to play, go to the practices and don't complain about it. It's that simple." Ian never complained about going to soccer practice again and enjoyed another 4 years of playing the sport. And we enjoyed watching . . . together . . . with the whole family.

---

When Bob and I split up, I had a 15 year-old Yorkie that I came into our relationship with. That was our only pet. So fortunately, we didn't have another painful decision to make about splitting up pets. Bob tolerated Bonito the Yorkie. But he was really a fan of bigger dogs at the time and didn't voice an interest in taking Bonito with him. After he established his own home and faced coming home to an empty house every night on alternating weeks, he decided to again explore pet ownership. As Ian's sixth birthday approached, it served up a perfect birthday present idea to Bob for his boy: Why not buy him a dog?

## Chapter 16
## Co-Pawrenting: It's Your Child's Dog

When Ian turned seven, Bob gave him a dog for his birthday – a beautiful purebred female Doberman pinscher puppy. Bob had done extensive research on area breeders and located a reputable one about two hours from our homes that had a litter maturing to six weeks perfectly timed with Ian's birthday. And so that is when they picked her up. Ian, being 7 years old, thought this was the best present he could ever get. And frankly, aside from maybe having a baby on one's birthday, I would have to agree that it was the best possible birthday present.

Ian with his Doberman Pinscher, Amber

Ian named the dog Amber for her pretty red-brown color. When she was only a few days old, the breeder had her tail cropped. Bob decided to proceed with the classic look by also having her ears cropped. I know some people disagree with doing this. But from a purely aesthetic standpoint, it makes for a beautiful profile. The process, however, does seem a bit medieval with bandages wrapped around the dog's ears to train them to stand. The whole process seemed to take forever – or at least a couple months – with Amber. As she grew, she was funny to watch as it seemed her limbs outpaced her ability to control them with her legs flailing about like rubber and occasionally tripping her up as she ran. But eventually, Amber trotted across the yard with the look of a champion thoroughbred horse in a dressage competition, majestic and graceful. Of course, this was the same dog that ran from her own poop. But, oh, how beautifully she ran from it!

However, Amber became a big dog who needed a lot of attention and exercise. Bob worked all day five days a week while Amber remained at home alone. As months passed and Amber grew, her powerful jaws found new and innovative ways to destroy Bob's belongings while he was gone. He tried moving her kennel to the basement in an attempt to minimize the destruction. But really, Amber was just lonely and acting out as a result. Bob faced a tough decision. What was he going to do with a dog that was destroying his house and was ultimately unhappy being alone all day?

One day, he told me he was going to see if his mom and stepdad would take her into their home. While this wasn't a horrible alternative, I felt it would still be viewed by Ian that Bob had gotten rid of his beloved pet. He had given away his birthday present. We both knew he'd be heartbroken by it. About this time, I started working at the house as a vocal coach and as such was home every day, only leaving to run errands and such. I had lost my 16 year old Yorkie the year before and was without a pet to keep me company on Ian's weeks with his dad. I was also a female living alone and thought the idea of a Doberman living in my home was sure to deter any potential house thieves. Who needs a security system when there's a dog that looks like it will tear your face off staring down would-be intruders? So I suggested that I try taking her. I had always been pretty good at training dogs to behave and felt confident that with me being there, most of her bad behavior would go away. At last, we had found a solution to avert a seven-year-old's heartbreak. Amber would simply move to Ian's other home.

I brought Amber to my house, and she seemed to feel instantly at home. She stopped the destructive behavior and provided me with much-needed companionship. She got to see her boy almost every day since Bob would drop Ian off and pick him up from my house before and after work. I had a nice backyard for her to run in, and a friend who was a professional dog trainer set us up with a remote electronic fence to keep her safely in the yard.

For the next twelve years we made countless memories with Amber. And we always enjoyed watching her run from her poop all majestic and graceful like a fine thoroughbred horse.

---

Planning ahead and sharing schedules are two of the quintessential ingredients to successful co-parenting. If you ever hope to plan a family vacation with your child after your divorce, you'll have a lot of other people to include in your list of considerations. So start your planning early and read the next chapter for tips on vacation planning for divorced parents and blended families.

## Chapter 17
## Vacations: Overcoming a Scheduling Nightmare

Vacations are absolutely about a thousand percent harder to plan for a family when divorce is involved than when it is not. Why? Well let's see . . . first you have to consider your schedule, the child's or your children's schedules if they are involved in sports or other activities, and the other parent's schedule. Then, if either parent is remarried or in a serious relationship, you have to consider the other partner's schedule and desires. If they, too, are divorced with children, you have to work around the schedule of the other parent and the other children's schedules. Then finally, if the said vacation is a group event based on years of tradition with a broader set of people, you may not even be at much liberty to dictate changes to the vacation schedule. And don't even get me started on blended families with stepchildren and their parents to consider in the mix. Seriously, scheduling a family vacation is among the most challenging of acts to pull off when all of these dynamics are simultaneously in play. Never mind accounting for the location, the weather, and travel arrangements. What a fricking nightmare!

*Teresa Harlow*

Still, scheduling family vacations has offered me one of my most profound lessons when it came to learning about compromise and also standing up for myself and my relationship with my son.

The years before I met my fiancé, Brian, were easier on vacation scheduling since I didn't have all the extra schedules to consider, and I could be more flexible on my end. Bob, on the other hand, never seemed to be in a position of setting his own schedule. As Ian entered high school and I met Brian, things became more challenging. Between Ian's marching band schedule and Bob's commitment to vacation with another family, we started to face some real challenges. Ian had about one month off from band each summer during which Bob and I would both scramble to fit in the family vacation. Brian's family had a 50-year standing tradition of vacationing in upper Michigan on the same week each July. Naturally, this week conflicted directly with the schedule Bob's friends had also kept for years. The first year we faced this dilemma, Ian spent the first week of a two week camping venture with his dad. I hung back in Columbus until Ian was driven back with someone who was returning early. Then I drove up with Ian to Michigan to join Brian and his family about four days later. This was a hectic grind for Ian and made me feel a bit awkward. I didn't like making him leave early from his vacation with his dad, and I didn't like us arriving late to our family vacation, either.

*Ian with Bob on vacation in the Carolinas*

## Happily Divorced

When the next year rolled around, we faced the same dilemma, and I didn't want to have the same awkward outcome. So I asked Bob if he could shift the dates of his vacation. At first, he couldn't believe I was asking him to do this since, in his mind, he had no say in the dates, and I could have picked any other week. But once I explained the long-standing tradition of Brian's family and the fact I could not, after 50 years, attempt to impose a drastic shift in the schedule, he agreed to talk to his contingent and negotiate a different set of dates. Had I not spoken up, Ian might have missed out on several years of enjoyment with his future stepsiblings and extended stepfamily at a wonderful location in northern Michigan wakeboarding, swimming, and enjoying these precious years with his mother at his side.

Ian and Teresa with Brian (taking photo) in Cancun, Mexico

As the years progressed, I came to appreciate Bob's quick rectification of the vacation schedule as our family vacation became the victim of many scheduling casualties on Brian's side of the blended family equation. Every year, it seemed there was some activity that his daughter or son absolutely couldn't bear to miss and that would inevitably interrupt our vacation schedule, but as stepparent, I simply didn't have the same influence over this situation and all too frequently had to just grin and bear it. We must all choose our battles carefully.

So next time you're planning the family vacation, I have a few suggestions that may help planning to go more smoothly.

1. Plan ahead

    I'm sorry, but you need to concede your spontaneous nature if you expect things to go smoothly in this department. If that bothers you, I'll just ask you to consider if you like it when people spring things on you and impact your schedule without even thinking about how it might affect your life. So be kind and discuss the plan even if it's just the dates, as soon as you know them. That way, if there are conflicts to overcome, you can start resolving those issues now and head into your vacation relaxed as nature intended it.

2. Be flexible

    Yeah, I know. This one is hard because when I say "flexible," it may require you bending over backwards to make everything work out. But don't assume your large group, ex-spouse, or new companion is inflexible on dates. Explain your circumstances rationally to decide on the best dates that will present the least conflicts for everyone.

3. Stick up for your relationship with your child

    It's important to understand that when I say be flexible, that doesn't mean you should always give in to the ex-spouse and forego your vacation desires. If your conflicts are impassible year after year, suggest alternating. One year he gets his way and the next year you get yours. If this doesn't work, ask him for suggestions that don't require you being the only one to compromise. If this still doesn't work, you may have to be a little more assertive with the situation by expressing to the ex-spouse that all you really want is to spend a nice family vacation with your child and to make sure he gets to do the same with his dad. When the father sees that you are trying to consider him in the equation, he may back off or offer up reasonable solutions. If not, then you're probably struggling with your ex on a number of fronts, which requires a deeper conversation to get on a path that is more harmonious.

4. Remember what you really want

   What do I mean by this? Well, you don't want to get your way if this means your child will be left feeling awful about the situation. If your child or children are going to miss a monumental family event or once-in-a-lifetime experience by not joining a particular vacation, you'll want to do everything in your power to ensure they are included. Later on when the whole family is sitting around the Thanksgiving dinner table together reminiscing about that time in Paris, your child will be part of the family story.

   You don't want to get your way if it means destroying future prospects of cooperation with your ex-spouse or others with whom you are still connected within his group. Like so many other circumstances in our lives, we have to think of others and the impact our actions have on them and decide if the way they feel as a result of these actions makes us happy or not. If your child isn't happy, you're probably not going to be, either. So this may mean that if your child could go to Disney with dad or on the annual family camping trip with you one year, they might enjoy Disney more, and you should probably let them choose Disney guilt-free. Now if this happens every year, to me it signals that the other parent is manipulating the situation intentionally and that's not cool, either. When this happens, refer back to #3.

In any case, be sure not to turn the family vacation into a weapon used to guilt your child or your ex, to win favor in your child's eyes, or worst of all, to deny them unforgettable childhood experiences just so you get your way.

---

Earlier in the book I mentioned our son's passion for music. This passion served up countless opportunities for Bob and me to find common ground upon which to build a successful co-parenting relationship. Not only did we both love our son but we both loved music. Read on to learn how we leveraged this common interest to support our son, continue our bond as parents, and enjoy time together all at the same time.

## Chapter 18
## *Nurturing a Child's Talents: Our Budding Musician*

From before the time when Ian entered this world, I fully expected to give birth to a musician, or at least a person that had a deep appreciation and keen aptitude for music. From the time I was four years old, I realized that I had a strong singing voice and was able to match pitch with great precision. I had dabbled in music over the years never setting aside my fear enough to really go after a career as a musician.

This dabbling persisted after Bob and I met when, one night out early in our relationship, we found ourselves at a Japanese karaoke bar. Yeah, I know – very stereotypical. After enduring renditions of various American pop standards crooned by old Japanese men, I decided to infuse something different. So I asked the person running the karaoke to queue up "Hopelessly Devoted to You," an Olivia Newton-John song from the *Grease* movie soundtrack.

Until this point, Bob had only heard me sing a little in the car. But when I hit the chorus and belted out the melody with all the power that came so easily to me, I leaned right over Bob's shoulder to emphasis the shock he was about to get. Belting the words "But now . . ." I glanced at Bob, who was both shocked and delighted to hear me bare my soul into the room. Bob and his friends were very impressed, and I once again was reminded I had something special to share with this world in the way of music. Over the next five years, with Bob's encouragement, or one might even say *insistence*, I hopped up with friends' bands and eventually became the lead singer in a couple of local cover bands. But even the free drinks and extra cash rewards fell short of what I thought my potential was.

Meanwhile, I toiled away in corporate America building a stable career so that we could enjoy a comfortable life while my soul languished dreaming of something greater. At this point, Bob and I had turned our thoughts and efforts toward starting a family. So after two long years and nearly giving up on our fertility, I decided to up the ante one more time.

The band I was singing with played two nights of shows at a dive bar on the north end of Columbus – a place I wouldn't dream of going to had we not been playing. That's not to say I let our friends use this as an excuse not to show up. It was my birthday that Saturday. I was in my mid-twenties and still had a relatively strong ability to recover quickly from over indulgence. Ah, those were the days!

Completely exasperated by my inability to get pregnant, I conceded that it was probably never going to happen. I was due to start my period and go through the disappointment yet again for a 25th straight month. So instead of facing that, I got hammered Friday and then proceeded to take it up a notch on Saturday with several shots of Tequila. Then I climbed up on a table and ripped off a drunken and very appropriate-to-the-moment rendition of Shelly West's country music tune "Jose

Quervo," and finished by doing who knows what else on stage in what could only be described as a blackout.

That Sunday, I lost a day of my life, so hung over that I don't think I ever left the bed. But this wasn't my first rodeo. I knew I'd feel better as soon as enough time had passed and my body had purged all the toxins and healed itself from the incredible pollution which I had inflicted upon it. Then Monday came, and oddly, I was still hung over. I thought this was really weird. Sure, I had drank too much – but a two day hangover? Come on! I didn't think it rose to *that* level of bodily destruction. Then it dawned on me: I was about 3 days late for my period. I became both instantly panicked and cautiously excited as it occurred to me that I might have really done it this time. I might be pregnant *and* I might have just poisoned my unborn child with a deluge of shitty tequila as well.

By about noon, I decided to do a home pregnancy test just to see if it was possible that I was carrying a hungover embryo. The test was positive. Oh, my God! None of them had *ever* come back positive. Better make a doctor's appointment to see if this is for real. I phoned my doctor, went in that afternoon, and they confirmed my pregnancy. I went home, and unable to contain myself, decided I better detox anything alcoholic left in my system and cleanse my bloodstream as fast as possible. So I went for a two-mile run and drank about a gallon of water. Then when Bob got home, I shared the news with him that he was going to be a dad, and from that moment on, really, I always expected I would give birth to a son and probably a musician.

About 19 weeks later, the son was confirmed on ultrasound. At that point, we began to contemplate names. Bob requested that the first name be Robert as he and his father before him. I was fine with this but proclaimed, "Ok, but I'd like to pick the middle name. I'd like it to be *Ian*, and also, we have enough Bobs and Bobbies in this family. So I'd like him to go by his middle name. It is the name of a really attractive and cool guy I knew during high school. Plus it's a great rock and roll name, right?" Bob, not convinced by my first argument, was totally on board with the latter and proceeded to recite the names Ian Anderson (Jethro Tull), Ian Gillan (Deep Purple), and Ian Astbury (the Cult & The Doors) as supporting examples of our case. And so Ian's musician fate was sealed with an appropriate name.

Bob and I went to five concerts together in those nine months during my pregnancy – more than I had in any other similar period of time in my life. Nurturing my little musician had already begun. Steely Dan, Dream Theater, and Lenny Kravitz were among Ian's prenatal inspirations.

After his birth, Ian's earliest exposure to music came in the form of mommy's serenades. As it turned out, after I returned to work and Ian was about three months old, I had to sing the song *Material Girl* live at a work function. So as I practiced singing the song, Ian heard it a lot as he laid on the changing table. He really liked that *Madonna* tune back in the day. Flash-forward to when Ian was about 9 months old in the back of my Honda Civic in the car seat, and a new style of rock had taken America by storm – Grunge! *Stone Temple Pilots'* "Interstate Love Song" came over the radio, and I glanced in the rearview mirror to catch Ian "air-drumming" in perfect time to the rhythm of the music. Wait. What? Is he going to be drummer? No way. My most challenging relationships in every band I had been in were always with the drummers. I couldn't have possibly given birth to one. Of all band members, they were always the ones I had conflicts with. So yeah, of course he would be a drummer because getting along with a drummer was apparently a life lesson for me.

*Happily Divorced*

And so it began. First with a plastic baby drum kit from Grandma and Papaw on his first birthday, then upgraded to a metal kit with paper heads on birthday #2, proceeded by a junior size full drum kit with real hardware and heads at age 4. Apparently Grandma and Papaw thought they were getting some kind of revenge on their son. Little did they know that it was just what daddy wanted. It didn't bother mommy, either, since I

had remained in local cover bands until about six months into my pregnancy and took it up more aggressively once Ian turned a year old. At that point, I became the lead singer in a local band we called

*Random Order.* We always liked to snicker about the oxymoronic quality of the name. Anyway, Ian had been subjected to listening to my band practices from the age of one. So when he showed interest, it thrilled me.

I continued singing in local cover bands for several years past the point of our divorce. And while this was a passion, it was a hard choice

because there were many weekends when it was my weekend with Ian but I had a show and ended up asking Bob and Brandi to keep him, had Ian stay with a friend, or got a babysitter. Now I wasn't only missing out on half of his life. I was missing out on the other half, too.

During this phase, Bob and Brandi were what I would call apprehensively supportive. Honestly, I totally understood where they were coming from. As I neared my 40th birthday, things began to wind down for me. I was finally feeling more and more frequently like I'd rather not spend my weekend in a bar while my son spent time with other people. And it wasn't like we were writing original material. So we weren't on the brink of a record deal. My son, on the other hand, was in fifth grade by this time and decided to start his own rock band. I suspended my band membership for the foreseeable future preferring instead to put my energy into helping Ian to grow his dream.

At the tender age of 10, the boys' instruments were quite literally bigger than they were. But they had it all figured out. I remember Ian telling me one day that he wanted to be in a band when he grew up but he added, "No offense mom, but we're going to write original music." I told him sweetly that I wasn't offended by his statement. Let's face it. Besides Weird Al Yankovic, there are very spotty examples of unknowns making it solely on the basis of covering someone else's material – Nashville singers aside, of course. And even Weird Al changed the words up to make them original.

There were five band members in *Flame Brain* as Ian's first band was called. Ian played drums, of course. Ian's best friend Yuji, whose parents had moved here from Japan a year or two before as part of his father's job transfer played bass; Blair, another of Ian's good friends from school, who had moved here from Louisiana about the same time

*The original boys of Flamebrain included Ian (front row), Blair, Joe, and Travis. Yuji joined shortly after this photo was taken.*

as Yuji, played guitar. He was the one I saw as the risk-taker of the group – you know, the one that makes every parent a little nervous for fear of what physically dangerous activity he may influence your child to partake in. Travis, Ian's dear friend since they played t-ball together as four-year-olds also played guitar. Travis, was the one who showed the earliest signs of being girl-crazy – and with his looks, the potential was there to get both him and at least a handful of girls into trouble. Finally, there was Joe, the smart kid who loved tech gadgets and who told me sometime while he was in middle school that he wanted to design computer hardware and figure out how to make it smaller and faster like Apple did with the iPhone right about that time.

At first, no one was sure what Joe was going to do in the band. Blair and Travis already played guitar, and Joe was ok for his age but was not very passionate about the idea. Then one day, he told me that he sang in the school chorus. Since none of the other band members were really showing stellar vocal prowess, I asked the boys the obvious question. "Why isn't Joe the lead singer?" With that, they decided to give him a shot. Joe ended up holding the position of lead singer for the duration of Ian's school days bands all the way through high school graduation.

With the first band lineup set, Ian set out on his journey as a musician. He organized regular band practices. And since I had some experience and owned a PA, I offered to mentor the boys and let them practice at my house. The truth is nothing could have been more thrilling for me. Of course, their first cover was the favorite first song of many a cover band, Deep Purple's "Smoke on the Water." I'm sure many of my musician friends can relate to this early experience. The boys proceeded to put together a full set of cover material. In sixth grade, they got the opportunity to play five songs at the middle school dance.

I asked one of my former guitarists to assist with some equipment needed for the show and to help the boys get properly tuned. As this newly formed possibly future phenomenon took the stage, I witnessed what can only be described as a Beatles-style audience response complete with swooning screaming tween girls. I was standing with all the band parents who were simultaneously overjoyed and laughing our asses off. It was, after all, not an airport, concert hall, or stadium. It was the middle-school cafeteria. But as lead singer, Joe – egged on by his older eighth-grade brother – stage-dived into the crowd, the boys' experienced that rush of acceptance and positive energy that so many musicians become addicted to. As they exited the stage after that performance, I remember crowds of students gathering around them as if Flame Brain was the biggest rock band in the world. The boys were all smiles and absolutely HOOKED!

Flame Brain continued to play throughout middle school at dances, benefits, band battles, and local restaurants. They wrote their first original song for a band battle in eighth-grade and took second place among a very crowded much older roster of players – much like the band from the School of Rock. Soon after that, they concluded that they had outgrown their band name and changed it to *Evadale Drive*, a name taken from a street in our neighborhood. How sweet and a pretty cool band name, too.

Amazingly, this band stayed together through the end of high school, going through good times and bad, often fighting like brothers, and sometimes facing challenges with bad choices that many teens make. I always reminded them to look out for each other and keep each other safe. I couldn't help but imagine that if they continued, it was inevitable that one day at some band performance somewhere someone would offer them something backstage while the parents weren't watching. So I had to instill in the boys some personal responsibility for each other's safety that I could only hope would ward off the worst of these dangers.

As band gigs continued, all of us band-parents were very supportive, each bringing something to the table. Not only was this our children's journey, it was ours as parents. Let's face it: It was the closest any of us were going to get to being rock stars. During these years, Bob provided a lot of opportunities for the band to play, bought sound equipment, and ran sound frequently for the band. He also brought consistent crowds of friends and family with him to the shows. Mike, Travis' dad, videotaped every show, editing and distributing copies to all band members and parents. Travis' mom, Anita, created countless posters, flyers, business cards, and press packs. She and Mike even created a second practice location in their house complete with another drum kit for Ian to use in their home. Blair's mom, Nikki, offered her photography skills and worked hard to keep her son on the straight and narrow. Mike and Melissa booked shows and helped with set-up and tear-down, striving to learn the proper technique for wrapping up miles of speaker, PA, and instrument cables. I was the consummate stage mom and assisted with everything from vocal coaching, advice on stage presence, and even attitude counseling (whether they wanted it or not). My motto for them was "check your ego at the door." Oh, and did I mention we all served as "roadies?" This is a cool term assigned to those who are charged with carting hundreds of pounds of gear up and down stairs, in and out of vehicles and setting it up at all the shows. It was so great when the boys were finally big enough to carry their own stuff.

There were many aspects of raising our young musician that required a great deal of shared parenting coordination including financing music gear purchases, paying for instrument lessons, managing schedules, riding together to shows, and sometimes discussing at great length the many little dramas that inevitably afflict all bands. I'm so glad Bob and I remained friends throughout these years so that we could offer the best version of support to our son, and rather than add stress to his events, work together to enhance his early musical experiences.

I guess I could write a whole book on my son, the aspiring musician, and maybe someday I will. I so look forward to the unfolding of his talent for the world to experience. May your rock name serve you well on your journey, Ian Harlow.

---

I am happy to say that Ian has not succumbed to the temptations that many musicians encounter. He finished school with high academic marks. He never got into drugs or alcohol before the legal age and even now is very responsible with his choices. When I look at what some parents have had to face with their children, I count my lucky stars that Ian has just been so easy on us. Still, he was a child, and like everyone, not perfect. So discipline was another topic we as co-parents had to master together to get the best results. I'll talk about our approach to discipline and some of the not-so-great examples I have witnessed among other co-parents I've observed over the years.

## *Chapter 19*
## *Discipline: A United Front*

Of all the parenting topics I cover, this one is central to why we needed to get this co-parenting thing right. I refused to let Ian be a casualty of his parents' choices. And I have to say, I think both Bob and I tackled the subjects of limits, responsibility, and discipline beautifully.

One of the saddest things I've witnessed in observing other divorce situations is the inability of divorced couples to effectively discipline their children and teach them how to make good life choices. The divorced parents become so fearful of the possibility that their child or children will reject them that they choose not to engage in any conversations that might jeopardize their relationships. I have seen it so many times: Fathers with limited visitation who can't fathom making even one precious moment with their children unhappy during the short hours they spend together; Mothers who buy their kids everything they ask for so that the children don't consider whether they may have more material rewards if they lived with Dad. On and on it goes. The child isn't given any responsibilities and is never told no. They are constantly showered with compliments on how great and beautiful they are and never denied anything. From a lack of household chores to never living without something simply because "mom said so," the kids of divorced parents frequently run the show.

You may be thinking, "So what, if everyone's happy all the time?" Is it so bad to have only positive interactions with your child? Frankly, YES! First of all, if *you* don't teach your children about things like washing the dishes and doing laundry, who do you think is going to do that? Or are you planning to supply your child with a staff of household servants after they move out? Or maybe you're ok with them wallowing in filth later on because they never learn the value of basic home cleanliness and how it can affect their physical and mental health. Could you be unwittingly raising a future hoarder to be featured on the cable series *Hoarders, Buried Alive*? Maybe you, too, were raised without being expected to help around the house and think this is just fine. After all, look at you. You turned out ok. But I bet if you think about it, you had more responsibilities than you are willing to admit, particularly since it may cause you to question your current course of action.

But this is about so much more than learning how to clean the house. What happens to a person who is never told *no*, denied anything, or challenged on his or her thinking? You got it! That child grows up to be a spoiled, self-serving narcissist, ill-equipped to deal with the real world where he or she will most certainly be told *no* by someone. There will eventually be someone who disagrees with him or denies her something desperately wanted. And you have failed to prepare your child or children for this event. They will be devastated and have no idea how to respond appropriately and productively to failure, going without, or having to think of others first.

So if you think the above is a lot of preaching from me without a lot of evidence that it doesn't have to be this way, read on to our experience. Of course, this will be easier to pull off if both parents share foundational values. This is probably more important in the areas of discipline, setting limits, and teaching responsibility than any other.

Remember when you first learned you were going to be a parent? If you're like me, you probably were struck simultaneously with profound fear and excitement at the prospect that you would be raising a human being that, with God's grace, would someday positively influence humanity. Sure, you may have dreamed of your child growing up to be famous or rich or beautiful. But I doubt anyone hopes her child grows up to be a self-absorbed jerk. So Bob and I were going to make damn sure we didn't raise one. Beyond the contribution of our DNA, this was our next most important responsibility.

When Bob and I divorced, I was fortunate enough to know that we shared very similar core values though there are nuances. Otherwise, we might have never gotten divorced at all. But we both took and still take the responsibility of parenting very seriously and personally. We both realize that while we want Ian to like us, liking us is not more likely because we give him everything he wants. We accept that it is our responsibility to teach Ian kindness, generosity, and accountability as well as to provide him opportunities to succeed in life. However, I have known many people who were seemingly given every opportunity to succeed by way of paid college tuition and financial assistance of all sorts but who still fell flat on their face precisely *because* it was given to them.

I grew up in a home where my dad had a convenient excuse to give me when he and mom didn't want me to have something: "We can't afford it," he'd say. It's a perfect alibi. Growing up, I always said to myself that when I had kids, I didn't want to have to tell them they couldn't have something because "we can't afford it." So I set out to make sure that wasn't going to be the case only to find out that it is much easier to say "We can't afford it" than it is to teach some more difficult life lesson to our child such as "You can't have it because it is bad for you. If you simply say you can't afford it, that pretty much shuts down all debate. So in one sense, it's brilliant because the end is the same, and maybe the child is less distressed than if you tell her she can't have something because you think it is too extravagant. The next thing you might hear is some variant of, "Am I not important enough for you to part with your precious money over?" Let the parental guilt trip begin.

So as co-parents, what strategy of discipline would Bob and I employ? We could go with the convenient lack of funds explanation or we could also take the route that many of our parents and grandparents took before them. They said, "No." The end. If we dared to ask why, we got the ever popular "because I said so." And if we dared challenge this reasoning, we might well have ended up grounded, or worse yet, slapped, spanked, or even beaten,

I like to think of my personal approach, which mostly worked, as a little more balanced and provided our son with the lessons he needed later in life. I said *no* when I thought something was not in his best interest AND I offered a simple explanation in matter-of-fact terms. While I didn't allow a full-fledged debate on the subject, I did listen to what he had to say in response as an opportunity to confirm whether or not he understood my rationale – even if he didn't agree with it. He didn't need to. I was most concerned with his wellbeing and conveying to him that regardless of anything else, my priority was to protect him from harm of any kind, and of course, to not raise a jerk. This was important stuff even when it made me unpopular with him. It's the risk I had to take. I also knew it was what Ian both wanted and expected from me. And this required setting limits. So I set limits and stuck to them, and I shared those limits with Bob. He did the same. We would sometimes negotiate on the finer details such as video game ratings or curfews. And we didn't agree on all these details, either. But our foundation was the same. First priority – protect Ian from harm – physical, mental, and emotional. Second priority – don't raise a jerk.

Ian and I most certainly had our negative days – some because he pushed it and some because maybe I had a bad day at work, was too exhausted to think straight, or was PMS-ing. But these were invaluable exercises in communication, problem-solving, self-control, and compromise for Ian. They also offered these benefits to me as well. But this was *his* first rodeo, and I was the clown protecting him from being trampled by the bull.

But what do you do when you and your child simply can't get to common ground? When you're still married to the other parent, you can call him in for reinforcement. But what about when you're divorced? Can you still do that? You can, but you have to be very secure in your relationship with the ex. Calling in the other parent for reinforcement isn't a workable plan if he or she's going to use the event against you, either to badmouth you to the child or to build a case that you are an unfit parent. Unfortunately, for many divorced parents this is the reality. But for others, it's simply a fear, a personal insecurity. If your ex-spouse has not brought legal action against you seeking to reduce your parenting time or interaction with the kids, you probably have a good chance of being able to partner with him or her in matters of discipline. See it as an opportunity to find common ground – a precious commodity among divorced co-parents.

There was a time during Ian's middle-school years where he and I had the most trouble communicating. I think he was sure he was being judged by everyone, including me, all the time. Like any other pre-teen, Ian lacked confidence and at the same time felt compelled to wield control over something, anything, even if that was a heated conversation with mom. Now, I'm going to say something I'm sure some of you will not like and maybe disagree with. But it's what I believe based on my own personal experience and observations. Children fear dad more than mom, at least in a physical-harm sense, that is – even for those kids who have never so much as been tapped on the behind for a transgression. Sure, mom can make you feel like crap in words, but you won't bleed or lose a limb from it. So the pain she can inflict just doesn't carry the same fear factor as the potential damage dad can do with that extra weight and muscle to throw at you – even if dad has never touched you. I know this because I felt this way.

My dad had never laid a finger on me, but at one point during my teens, I pushed him too hard, and he grabbed both of my arms and shook me – not violently at all but more like he was trying to wake me up. And wake me up he did! It scared the hell out of me, not because it hurt but because it reminded me that he had the capacity to hurt me if he chose to. With that, my human survival instinct kicked in and forced me to shut my smart mouth. I'm sure there are exceptions where the mom is more physically intimidating than the dad. But I'd venture to say that with dad's deeper voice and larger stature, most kids can't battle the human instinct to protect themselves from physical harm, so they acquiesce to the one who is physically superior to them.

After arguing with Ian for several hours on this particular day about helping out around the house and him doing everything in his power to fight me on the point, I had enough. We were getting nowhere. I don't really remember the details of our actual argument. But I do remember feeling like we had devolved into a circular conversation that was simply not going to resolve without a radical change in strategy. So I called Bob and asked if he would talk to Ian. Bob didn't hesitate and came over to my house immediately. He laid it on the line with Ian and told him he was not to talk to me ever again in that tone or manner. He reinforced my points telling Ian that mom was right and that he needed to do what I said. In short, Bob was being a good father. I don't really get why this was so effective. Maybe it had nothing to do with the male versus female presence at all. Maybe it was simply the fact that bringing the other parent in tipped the opinion scale. Once Ian saw that Bob and I were on the same side, he realized he was outnumbered and was not going to win this one. So he conceded, and life returned to normal for everyone. Good for us. We didn't raise a jerk!

Bob, Ian, and Teresa at Ian's National Honor Society Induction ceremony

## *A Son's Perspective*

I do like to think I'm not a jerk. And I know my parents are not jerks either. They are both good people--amazing people, really. They are kind, generous, loving, responsible, respectable . . . the list could go on for pages. They raised me on the basic universal premise, "Treat others the way you want to be treated." The Golden Rule. Karma. Even when I would get in arguments with my mom, they would always boil down to whether or not this principle was being respected. I had consistent discipline from both parents in both homes growing up. This can even be rare from parents in the same home. I had friends who had a strict parent and a chill parent. How is a person supposed to learn anything after hearing two completely different answers to the same question from two seemingly reliable sources? They don't, and it causes issues for them later in life. Consistency is the name of the game when teaching someone anything. And my parents accomplished just that.

---

As separate-family-life continued, there were many times I simply knew that Bob was my best choice to turn to for help. There were also times when Bob turned to me for help. In these times of need, Bob and I chose to support one another as any friends would. Knowing we could count on each other was an important core principle to build a solid, trusting co-parenting relationship.

## Chapter 20
## Helping Each Other: Divorced Parents Do This Too

So I guess I could have started with this topic because really, this might very well be our secret sauce. But then if you knew that, you might not have read all the other chapters, right? And what a waste that would be. Bob and I have consistently and willingly helped each other through big life events and the little things ever since our divorce. At first, I think Bob would have probably rather not helped me. He was very angry with me, which is to be expected. But he was the bigger person, putting his feelings aside to make sure his son had a comfortable home to live in with his mom. He gave me a basic set of tools so that I could pound in a nail or screw together a piece of furniture. He bought and installed a high-end bathroom shower door from his business in Ian's bathroom. And he was consistently there to pick Ian up, drop him off, and spend time with him on a regular schedule without fail or complaining.

I can't tell you how many times I've asked Bob to borrow a tool or small appliance, costume, or anything else I might need but didn't have. If I needed a referral for anything – and I mean anything – Bob would always know a guy. In fact, I'm pretty sure Bob is the consummate "I know a guy" guy. Whether it is a painter, plumber, mechanic, or limo driver, Bob knows a guy. And he always invited me to use his name. "Tell them I sent you, and you'll get a good deal," he would say. There was never any hesitation or trepidation. Every request was readily accommodated without ever making me feel like I owed him something or that he had something over me, which is probably a good thing since I seem to have fewer things he needs, or maybe it's just because he has everything and knows everyone. But if there was something, I gladly shared my stuff and my referrals – need a musician or a psychic? I know some of those. I always felt good when I could offer him something he needed.

Besides being there with the "things" and the referrals, we were there to help each other through life's ups and downs, too. I'll admit I didn't help him move. But I did help move a lot of sound gear and music instruments between our homes. I babysat his daughter when he and Brandi had somewhere to go. I've gone to every viewing of every relative of Bob's whom I knew that have passed since we split – even one that I didn't know very well. I've offered help to his parents anytime they've hit physical and emotional challenges in their lives as well.

And when Bob got in a very bad motorcycle accident in the spring of 2016, I got up as soon as I received the text and never went back to bed. I went to the hospital to see him twice. I consoled his worried mom and sister and ate dinner with them (or actually watched them eat) in the hospital cafeteria. I talked to his stepdad the day after the accident and let him talk me through a play-by-play of the entire thing, which obviously he wanted to tell someone. Being a former state highway patrolman, Dick spared no details. It only took about 45 minutes for him to recount it all. During the days after Bob was able to return home from the hospital, I went to his house to visit him just to let him know I cared and was there for him. I told Brandi I'd help with whatever she needed – let out the dogs, bring the two of them dinner, take Gracie, anything. That's how you treat friends. You don't judge them. Ok, privately, you might. But hopefully you'll keep those thoughts to yourself and set them aside. You help them get through difficult times and realize it could just as easily be you in the situation. You are there for them and their families and offer your support.

Finally, and probably most germane to the topic of this book, we helped each other to be better parents. We talked about the issues parents deal with, especially the difficulties our son might be going through and how best to deal with them and help him. How to cover the Christmas list? How to pay for an expensive gift? How to help him get along better with neighbor kids? What sports should Ian try? How do we best support our aspiring musician? Who will go to curriculum night? Who's going to talk to the coach? And of course, we could gush all day long to each other about how wonderful our son is without annoying the other person. You really can't do that with a non-parent. Not even a stepparent past a certain point.

If you're reading this book because you are recently divorced or because you are not having a "happily divorced" experience, you may find all of this to be a lot to take on in your particular situation. All I can offer you is to remember the Golden Rule – the same one our parents taught us. *Treat others as you want to be treated.* I promise you even if it feels uncomfortable, the dividends of a positive relationship, and moreover, positive parenting experience for you and happy childhood for your offspring is *so* worth a bit of discomfort now and then. After all, it will certainly be less uncomfortable than when you lived in the same house with your ex.

Thank you, Bob, for always lending me your stuff and for being there for me. Mostly, thank you for being a great dad and talking to me about concerns you had as we raised our son. I know he is better off now because we worked together.

---

Lending me his stuff wasn't the only loans Bob made to me. As divorced couples, you may think you've escaped the idea of having to consider the finances of your ex. But as long as kids are involved, you really have to think about how everything that happens to one parent can affect the children's lives as well. Next up, I'll talk about the many ways our finances affected one another and how we managed it.

## *Chapter 21*
## *Finances After Divorce: Still a Joint Venture*

You may think that after you divorce, your financial lives will be severed as well. Not so. "What?" you say. Why is that? Simple: If you have kids together, whatever your ex-spouse and you achieve or don't achieve financially will impact your children's lives. So if you think your times of fighting about money are over, they probably aren't. And even if you don't fight about money, your spouse's choices will affect your choices and vice versa whether you like it or not.

For some, this plays out in the form of failed child support payments or the inability – or maybe even unwillingness – to pay half on basic expenses such as childcare, school supplies, clothing, etc. For most of Ian's youth, this wasn't the case for us. Bob and I were both gainfully employed. And we were both very generous with our son and interested in him having a balanced experience at both homes. However, there were a couple of occasions where each of us made choices that impacted the other's finances.

For me, it was this unquenchable thirst to be self-employed and run my own business. After 15 years of grinding it out, I grew tired of corporate America, job eliminations, and re-orgs that led to multiple lay-offs for me. If you've ever heard anyone say they got "RIF'd," that's an acronym for Reduction in Force. Basically, you go to work one day and they tell you that your job is going away, and they don't have another one for you.

I was RIF'd four times in five years during my "tour of duty" at a large bank in central Ohio. Every time, I was assured that it had nothing to do with the results I got or the quality of work I did. It was just one of those top-down decisions, and I was the collateral damage of being "below the line" of those being kept for one reason or another. In each of the first 3 times, I was able to find another position elsewhere within the company and took on a new job that matched my skills and experience. In 1999, I landed a job within our Internet banking group. The Internet was just coming into its own at that point, and I really enjoyed the types of cutting-edge technology I was learning. I felt as if I had finally landed in a place within the company that I could call home for quite some time. I was a little tired of chasing my career and really just wanted to be part of this new technological movement, deepen my knowledge of it, and become an expert.

Then 9/11 happened, and the world changed. Suddenly, financial institutions were cutting back on staff. There was also a new emotional, if not religious, awakening which affected how people viewed their lives. Suddenly, we all realized that tomorrow was not guaranteed. It could all literally come crashing down around us in an instant. And really, it didn't matter how you were living your life; it could all be taken from you without warning and through no fault of your own. So as our country began to recover, many of us realized that we should probably live our dreams now. Every time I think about 9/11, my mind goes to all those people who set out to work that day at their corporate jobs. It was a beautiful, bright and sunny Tuesday with perfectly blue skies. Someone just like me had arrived at work, gotten their first cup of coffee, sat down

## Happily Divorced

at their computer, and began tackling their day's work. They probably chatted with a few coworkers, maybe sharing funny stories about a recent *Friends* episode before all hell broke loose. They expected their day to unfold as it always did. For some, they were living the dream, making big money on Wall Street and going home to a nice house somewhere on Long Island. But through the plethora of post-9/11 stories that were told by survivors, you could feel a shift taking place. There were a lot of people who said that the attack changed them and how they looked at their lives. It changed their priorities and how they chose to spend their time. People changed careers opting to pursue their passions. Many focused more on their families. Corporations began to honor life-work balance. And I found myself RIF'd once again.

At this point, I was really sick of doing my best work, giving up countless hours and days of my own time only to further the interest of a corporation that saw me as nothing more than a salary number on a page that they needed to eliminate. By now, I was 35, divorced, the mother of an 8-year old, and wanted desperately for him to grow up seeing a parent pursue her dream and make a living out of it. As he was already expressing a desire to be a musician, I felt the need to be a role model for him to follow his dreams and not end up in a safe career by accident or because everyone told him it was what he "should" do. I've always told him what he "should" do is what makes him happy. So while I could have probably found another role within the bank yet again, I felt betrayed and also felt the urgency to start living my dreams immediately. So instead, I took some time off to decide what kind of business I might want to start. I used the 3 months of severance pay I received to decide on and plan my future career.

I briefly considered becoming a bridal planner. I had spent most of my childhood after school and on weekends in my mom's bridal shop and had planned my own wedding about a thousand times as a sort of fantasy exercise, selecting my designer wedding dress and bridesmaids' dresses, picking out invitations, choosing a cake, and, of course, reading up on all the best honeymoon spots. I helped my mom with every aspect of her business at one time or another. I truly had a wealth of knowledge to start with and created my business plan and bride's organizational workbook within 3 months. There was only one real problem here. I did NOT want to spend every weekend of my existence at a wedding. In fact, when I stopped and thought about it, I really didn't like weddings that much anymore. Maybe I was just burned out on them. But I knew I couldn't be successful in such an endeavor if my heart wasn't in it. So after being interviewed by one couple who considered hiring me, I abandoned the entire concept. I sold off stock options I had received while working at the bank and funded another 4 months of contemplation. Then I ran out of money.

I did have my band, though. I had just joined up with a new group of quality musicians, and we were starting to play shows for reasonable pay, which provided a good part-time income. But it would never support Ian and me living in the home we were in without other revenue streams.

My boyfriend at the time suggested that maybe I should teach people to sing. Hmmm . . . now that's an interesting idea!

*Happily Divorced*

*Teresa's cover band Scarlet. From left: Neil, Mike, Teresa, and Chris*

As the band income continued to tick up to a bit more than a part-time income, I got to work on the idea of teaching people to sing. I don't play piano or any other instrument. So to accompany students, I bought a karaoke machine, used my small-room band PA system, and took six months of piano lessons, which got me to the point that I could pound out scales and match pitches to coach students through troubled spots. With the help of my amazing girlfriends, I transformed my basement into a performance studio. To give the space a stage vibe , we spray painted the gas line piping black and hung black drapery put together with a boat-load of Stitch Witchery to close all the seams (Did I mention that in all that time in my mom's bridal shop, I never bothered learning to sew more than a button on a blouse?) I hand-painted fabric and we stretched it across the ceiling, and asked Bob to install a wall of mirrors for students to be able to watch themselves as they practiced their stage presence. With the studio done and piano lessons underway, I created a basic starter curriculum to offer and started telling everyone at my shows that I was offering private singing lessons. Voilà, *Scarlet Studio Vocal Coaching* was born.

I began taking on students, and before long had about 25 students a week, and I was covering all of my bills. At the same time, I pushed for more band bookings and started picking up acoustic shows with my guitarist to boost income in the summer when vocal student business dropped off. I thought I had everything pretty much in hand. But I didn't have a lot left over after paying bills. So when it came to paying for the extras for Ian – soccer gear, music lessons, instruments, and more extravagant clothing choices – I simply didn't have the funds to match Bob. Then there was the need to arrange for childcare for all those weekend and evening shows. I couldn't blame Bob if he resented my choices during this period. He was in a new relationship with his future wife, Brandi, and had always made the safe choices in life. During this entrepreneurial venture, I couldn't always pay half toward health insurance or the unexpected expenses for Ian and had built up a small debt with Bob. Oh, man, I never had been so much as 30 days late on a single bill, and I wasn't about to go there now. Plus, I really didn't want Brandi to think I was a deadbeat. I liked her and didn't care for the tension it was creating between us. I had been financially on my own, as had Bob, since the age of 18 and had only on one occasion when I was about 22 asked my parents for financial help. Bob and Brandi didn't have a lot of disposable income. So I didn't want to make this their problem. I apologized to them for falling behind on things, and as soon as I did have money to begin paying them back, I did so very quickly, prioritizing any of my own extras below that obligation.

You may be thinking "So what? You paid someone back. Big deal! You just did what any decent human being should do." And if that is what you're thinking, you would be right. Except ex's don't always treat each other like decent human beings or even with the same regard as they do their friends and family. They may even treat their mere

## Happily Divorced

acquaintances better than the mother or father of their child. It's unfortunate but true that in many cases, exes are regarded as the enemy. And to what end? Does it make life easier? No. In fact, just a little cooperation can go a long way to managing difficulties when times get tough. Honestly, if you think about it, all that treating your ex as the enemy will get you is . . . an enemy! Seriously, will that really help your situation?

It is not lost on me that Bob and Brandi didn't *have to* be patient with me when my finances took a nasty turn. They had no legal obligation to do so. Yet, they were. They only gave me a hard time on a couple occasions and it wasn't even that severe. They would say something in the course of conversation like, "Don't you think you should just get a job with a company again?" Still, they never made Ian go without simply because I couldn't cover my half. Whether they disagreed with my choices or not, they considered first and foremost what would be best for our son. Bob and Brandi could have made it much more uncomfortable for me. They could have done what some divorced parents do and talk me down to our son. But they didn't. They afforded me cooperation. And because they did, I was motivated by this spirit to make decisions considering how my finances affected not only our son, but Bob and Brandi as well.

You may be asking, "Why did you concern yourself with your ex-husband's financial wellbeing? " Let me be explicit because this really could be a watershed moment in terms of how you think about an ex-spouse: If I didn't fix my financial woes, it burdened him and his wife, whether they liked it or not. And if their finances were impacted, so too was the standard of living my son enjoyed in their care. Even if they would have chosen to play hardball with me, give me a hard time, or withhold their assistance, it wouldn't have fixed the real problem, which was my lack of money. It would have only created another problem – discord between us and injury to our future efforts to cooperate on many other matters as co-parents. Bob and Brandi chose wisely not just for me and Ian, but through their efforts to maintain an ongoing positive relationship with me, they actually helped themselves. How about that? Be considerate of your ex and *your* life improves. Oh, sweet karma!

Eventually, right before I completely ran out of money to cover even basic living expenses, I contemplated making a difficult but fiscally responsible choice. I could go back to my corporate career. While I loved running the studio and coaching people to sing, not only had it become a financial burden to all of us, it conflicted heavily with the time I had with Ian. Since most of my students wanted appointments after work or school, it meant that pretty much every day when Ian would walk in from school around 3:00 in the afternoon, my lessons were usually just starting for the day and would continue through 9:00 or 10:00 p.m. each night. We couldn't have dinner together, and it was difficult for me to make it to soccer practices or other after-school functions. Fortunately, Ian was a good student and didn't need my help on school work very often. Still, looking back, I would like to have been more involved in what he was doing. To this day, guilt myself about not volunteering more at Ian's school like I'm sure all the other mothers did. So the schedule wasn't working. The finances weren't working. And I was feeling growing guilt from missing mommy moments I knew I only had one shot at. In 2004, after living the dream life of a professional musician and entrepreneur for a little over two years, just the right opportunity to hop back into my old career surfaced, and I returned as a consultant for 5 years to the corporate grind.

Then the great recession of 2008 happened and virtually all consultants in "non-essential" roles were cut. You have got to be kidding me! I had just finished two consecutive large projects with enormous success that resulted in many of my clients receiving awards for the work I had led (consultants don't get these rewards. Their reward is the business and income it generates). I'm really not sure which tore down my self-esteem more: Getting laid off multiple times even when I was getting stellar results, or knowing my role was *nonessential*? Well, crap. Now what?

We were now entering 2009. At that point, I faced the daunting reality that I simply may not be employable given my current skills and experience. Further, I felt I may not have been suited to work for others. And even if I were, there were no available jobs in my field. So I walked back out of the Dilbert comic strip once again and set out to conquer the world of natural food and holistic health, a subject that had become a personal mission for me as I healed myself of many physical ailments that pharmaceuticals either failed to address or actually caused.

Once again, I embarked on starting a business from scratch with little money in savings to cover startup costs or general living expenses while this thing got off the ground. Thankfully, my business partner (with whom I'd been working for the preceding two years) and I had laid some of the business foundation. We had formed an LLC, created a business model that we were testing, and drafted a business plan that suggested we could both make about $200K annually with modest results. When I got laid off, I informed my business partner that I was going to go fulltime on our venture but would need his support. He agreed to keep his corporate job and front our working capital needs. Mind you, I still didn't have a plan to cover personal expenses beyond about 4 months. So my plan was to really hustle. And that I did. Except the one skillset which I needed most every day all day was sales. And that was supposed to be what my business partner brought to the table.

Now here I was the one with the time and energy but absolutely NO experience or desire to take on the role of salesperson. Yikes! Seriously, cold calling scared me to death. I hated to be disappointed and just couldn't face possible rejection. I continued to morph our business model to something I felt I could offer without really selling it *per se* – something that people would be willing to pay for, which also didn't require a lot of start-up money. I decided to become a personal wellness coach. But this plan didn't really work for my business partner who was neck-deep in responsibilities at his corporate job. He just didn't have the energy after his job each day to work on our business. For him, it was just an expense that wasn't producing a return. After a while, I suggested we talk about it. Since we had been friends long before the business, I told him that I really didn't want to destroy that and thought it best we part company on the business so that our friendship might survive. He accepted this and we ended our business partnership. The friendship still survives today.

I continued on my own as a wellness coach for another two and a half years. I had no income, but I did have stellar credit, and a lot of it. I also had started dating Brian, and when we hit the year and half mark, he agreed to move in to my home so we could share expenses. He was at my place all the time, anyway. So this seemed like a logical choice and removed the fear I had of losing our home. My car was paid off. Thank God! I continued to trim expenses as much as I could.

But there were still the business expenses to cover and the cost of raising my son. Again, I found myself burdening Bob and Brandi with picking up my slack. Again, they didn't say too much about it. Maybe this is because they had faith in me based on my past track record. I wouldn't leave them high and dry, and they knew it. I would pay my debts to them. And when I was again in a position, I would more than

*Happily Divorced*

cover my fair share of things. They may not have been so understanding had I not been so quick to right the situation in the past. I received their cooperation, consideration, and respect because I had given it to *them*.

Ironically, my lack of income during Ian's senior year in high school and first two college years set all of us up for significantly lower college expenses since he was deemed in financial need. Had I been making my corporate salary, Ian wouldn't have qualified for any of the need-based grants and scholarships he received. If he hadn't gotten that extra financial aid, both Bob and I would have been on the hook to contribute thousands more per year to the equation or been forced to saddle Ian with a lot more student loan debt. So from this perspective, my financial difficulties saved all of us thousands of dollars on college tuition. I guess I chose the best years to be broke.

I am so appreciative of the support that Bob and Brandi gave me during the lean years. And one awesome thing that did come out of it was I could be home to greet Ian after school almost every day throughout his high school years. I could make sure that after-school choices he made were better than the ones I had made as a teen home alone after school in the 80s.

Of the two of us, I certainly earned the award for financial woes. But when I emerged from these difficulties, I did try to make up for this. I paid for many things on my own that I never bothered to mention to Bob. They were things Ian needed or really wanted, and I just got them. When Bob had his motorcycle accident, I paid for Ian's college graduation cap and gown. I also bought Bob a set of Ian's graduation pictures and covered the cost of Ian's grad party at my house. I knew Bob was about to get hit with an avalanche of medical bills. The pictures and party expenses weren't that much, and Bob was focused on getting his life physically back on track. So I just covered it. As time went on, when larger expenses for Ian came up, I would front the money and tell Bob to pay me when he could. And there were things I just did on my own that I didn't expect to be reimbursed for. I'm sure Bob did such things, too.

Bob never obsessed too much about my financial difficulties. He afforded me his trust that I was doing the best I could. In return, I did the same. The point is that sometimes you do both big and small things for your ex or in consideration of your ex because your child's other parent is inextricably part of your family financial tree. In this way, you are connected to each other and affect each other long after the divorce is finalized, and most likely for the remainder of your lives to one degree or another. So do you want the expenses associated with raising your child to be the reason you can't deal cooperatively with each other on many fronts? Will resentment make the situation better, or would a little consideration sow the seeds of harmony between you?

I truly believe that the reason Bob and I were able to successfully navigate difficult financial periods was because we each established that we could be trusted by the other. We both continued to care about how our decisions affected the other. We also realized that our finances were at least somewhat bound to each other by our co-parenting arrangement whether legally specified or not.

---

We had come a long way on our journey as co-parents, managed to save our family, re-stabilized our finances, and had continued our friendship. As Ian's school years wound down, we found ourselves again at a point of transition. And *Toy Story 3* was up for Best Picture. How appropriate!

## Chapter 22
## Graduation Part 1: High School Comes to an End

Ah, graduation. I'm guessing parents with more than one child view high school graduation differently than those of us with an only-child. If it's the oldest child, it's a new experience for the parents. If it's the youngest, it's the last time they'll ever do it. They probably also think about the fact they will soon be one step closer to empty-nest freedom. If you're the parent of a single child, it's a little different. Every experience is the first and last time you'll have it. You get no do-overs. No mulligans. No screwing things up, learning from mistakes, and getting it right the next time. It's really a lot of pressure. Then there are the married parents who look forward to having an opportunity to rekindle their relationship. Maybe even restore the romance they experienced with one another pre-child. For me, the single mom of an only child, it represented the end of so many things I loved about being a mom and co-parent that I would never get to experience again.

First there was the graduation itself. I started dreading that about halfway through Ian's junior year when he began visiting colleges and taking college entrance exams. He was going to leave home. I wouldn't be able to be there for him when he finished his day. I wouldn't be able to make a healthy dinner for him. There would be no more high school football games or parades to see him perform at (not that there wouldn't be more performances in his case). The high school experience, which I once loathed, myself, but now looked back on fondly, was coming to an end for our son. My, how fast life goes by.

As for my relationship with Bob, there would be far fewer reasons for us to talk. Would this mean our friendship would fade? Would I never have the pleasure of hearing his funny tales or get to spend time with his family. Quite frankly, I was overwhelmed with sadness for about 18 months. I felt my worth and usefulness as a mom was fast diminishing. My identity was slipping away. I feared that many cherished relationships would simply fade into time, and I would be forgotten. This may all sound overly dramatic, but it really is what I felt.

Thankfully, Ian chose to attend college close to home. So by the time his second semester of his senior year of high school rolled around, I no longer had to consider what I might do if he chose to head off to Southern California or Florida. He would be able to drive 20 minutes or so from campus to home and I could do the same. What a relief!

The first senior event Bob and I jointly participated in was senior night during

## *Happily Divorced*

football season. Senior football players, cheerleaders, and band members were all honored and given an opportunity to walk across the field with their parents, have their pictures taken at the other side, and be introduced over the PA to the audience. Bob and I never considered doing it any other way than together. In fact, I might even go as far as to say that we inspired other divorced parents to do the same. After all, many of them had watched Bob and me as co-parents over the course of Ian's entire academic career. They saw this as possible for them, too. I like to *think* we inspired a few others, anyway. As we proudly took the field together, we arrived at the other side for the official sanctioned photo-op. No, we didn't do anything crazy or embarrassing – although thinking about it now, that would have been hilarious. Instead, we posed respectfully for another snapshot of the three of us together to take forward through our lifetime of memories.

Throughout Ian's senior year of high school, Bob and I attended band concerts, rock-band performances, and senior banquets with our new partners, with grandparents, and all of us always sitting together.

Last on the list was to create a memorable graduation experience for Ian – one that both of our families could join in together. I wanted Ian to have a graduation party. I did not have one, and at the time, didn't miss it. But I realized not only did I miss out on marking this occasion in a special way, but I also missed out on gathering some much-needed cash for what comes next in life through presents offered by those in attendance.

In our case, the last thing I wanted was to make Ian split time between families during his celebration. And since we were all on such good terms and genuinely enjoyed each other's company, why shouldn't we hold one big joint celebration? Bob suggested we hold the party at his house since the backyard was better positioned to set up the tents

## *Teresa Harlow*

and tables for guests. Since we were only a quarter-mile apart as the crow flies, it would be easy enough for everyone to find Bob's if they did not know where Ian's "other home" was. We split the costs of food and decorations. And I was free to invite my friends and family to Bob's house, which I did without concern. Bob's wife, Brandi, helped with a lot of the details and with making sure we got our guest list together and invitations mailed on time. I created an invitation using several pictures arranged into a collage, and we jointly addressed and mailed them. I also created a couple of picture posters with snapshots throughout Ian's life, being extra-careful to make sure family members and friends from both sides were represented. I absolutely wanted everyone to feel like they were included in this great celebration and recognized for their significance in Ian's life. I would not have dreamed of doing it any other way. Contrast this with the experience of another father I know. In his case, the ex created posters that contained not one single picture which included dad. How sad. What did the daughter think when she looked at these? Did she think Dad was never there? Or did she recall perfectly how dad was always there and think that mom was just being petty and selfish. Kids aren't dumb. When parents take this kind of approach when dealing with the other parent, the child sees it and either is hurt by it or comes to believe this is an acceptable choice should they ever find themselves in the same position. Of course, it's possible that the mom just didn't give it any thought. This is unfortunately the path too many take when they divorce – simply failing to consider the feelings of not only the other parent, but of the child to whom that other parent is definitely important. Nice going, mom.

When graduation day arrived, we sat together at the ceremony and took pictures together afterward. Then we set out to create our everlasting memories of the graduation party. Bob's large local family contingent was there. And while my parents and other family members weren't there, all living out of state and unable to make the trip, I did invite Brian's family and several close friends and neighbors. So there was a reasonable balance representing both sides.

During the party, Bob and I were both careful to make sure we intermingled the groups, introducing those who didn't know each other and encouraging cross-over conversations, if you will. It was nice to see Ian so relaxed being able to enjoy himself and not worrying about having to leave to go to the other parent's celebration. He could do what all the other kids did and leave his own party to attend his friends' parties while the parent celebration continued. Ha!

---

With fewer reasons for obligatory communication, I felt a sadness settling in. Would I still be invited to spend time with Bob and his family for special gatherings? Would I see Sandy and Debbie and the rest of Bob's family anymore? Would they forget about me? I wasn't really sure how things would evolve once we became the parents of a college-age child. It would take real friendship that rose above our parental obligation for us to continue including each in the other's life.

## Chapter 23
## The Harlows: The Real Modern Family

When I typed this title into my book outline, I really wasn't sure what I was going to specifically write here, and even as the words hit the page, I'm not sure where they will take me. So let me start with this as I think it demonstrates the point.

When Bob's wife planned his 50th birthday party, she included me and Brian in the celebration. I contemplated whether or not to go for about a half second as I considered seeing all the old softball friends and their wives whom I really hadn't encountered much in the preceding 17 years. But just as I've always done, I considered the fact that what they thought wasn't as important as the fact that Brandi wanted us to be there. Plus, I relished another opportunity to spend time with my son and my beloved ex-in-laws. So I easily put my brief hesitation aside.

When I arrived at the party, it must have taken me twenty minutes to make it through the venue out to the back patio where the celebration was actually being held. I was greeted by countless members of Bob's family and friend group who made me feel right at home with all of them. Honestly, it was so genuine and well beyond an obligatory "hello" or "how have you been?" They showed real interest in talking with me and knowing how my life was going. I hope I returned the feelings of acceptance and interest in them that they afforded me. It was so comforting to feel so loved by those who for so long I felt I had fallen out of grace with when I left Bob. See, it is one thing to celebrate your child together and for everyone to focus on that. But when the "ex" shows up at the former spouse's birthday party, it is because they want to be there, not because it is expected due to parental responsibility. And it's true. I really did want to be there, and I really did enjoy it.

As I made my way to the patio, I came upon a poster board full of photos throughout Bob's life that Brandi had created. Ahead of the event, she had asked me for some snapshots that predated her; and I had supplied her with a stack. I wasn't sure how she would feel about including them. So I told her to use what she felt comfortable with and left it at that. I included pictures that Bob's mom had given me of Bob when he was in high school and pictures of him with Ian when he was a baby, toddler, and preschooler – all which predated Brandi. I also chose to include one other picture that probably was the most controversial choice if you were an outsider to our special relationship. It was a picture of Bob and me together after a softball game when I was about seven months pregnant. We both looked so happy and young and Bob had his hand on my pregnant belly. I really didn't know if Brandi would be willing to put this one in the collection she created for public viewing.

As I scanned the board, I didn't really look specifically for this picture because I had convinced myself to have no expectation and to harbor no judgment either way she went with that. But then my eyes locked on it, and I was filled with joy when I saw that this particular image made the board. See, not only did it represent the happiest time of our marriage and the impending birth of our only son, who is amazing, but it also was us in the element in which we had enjoyed so much fun with

*Happily Divorced*

friends celebrating softball wins at the local pub after the game. I had lost all those friends in the divorce, and many of them were there that night. Having that picture on the board made me somehow feel even more like a part of the celebration – a key orchestrator in the creation of our family 2.0 and a genuine friend – still! I probably spent more time

talking with Bob's friends that night than I had even when we were all hanging out at the pub after all those games. I was no longer a person separate from the group who was just tagging along. On that night, I was a member of the group.

As the party progressed, Bob asked that someone "take a picture of his modern family" and grabbed both Brandi and I to pose with him. It was a really cool feeling and a proud moment for both of us. I just love my real modern family!

---

Ian's college years flew by, and before we knew it, were planning his college graduation celebration. Then as the date approached Bob found himself in a fight for his life after a serious motorcycle accident only two weeks before.

## *Chapter 24*
## *Graduation Part 2: Our Boy is a College Grad*

The date was May 7, 2016 when Ian graduated from Capital University in Bexley, Ohio with a bachelor's degree in Music Technology. I am so proud to be able to say that. It is something neither his father nor I can claim. Yeah, we're part of the so-called "uneducated" class joined in company by Steve Jobs, Bill Gates, Mark Zuckerberg, Michael Dell, and a host of other highly successful individuals who don't have college degrees. Bob and I may not be gabillionaires, but we've both managed to achieve comfortable incomes for ourselves. In spite of *us* overcoming our degree-less disadvantage, I didn't want Ian to be strapped with the same. What parent does? We all hope to save our children from making the same mistakes we did. It doesn't always work out, but we have to try. And quite honestly, given Ian's chosen profession, that piece of paper may not be all that. But the experience of being a college student, learning to interact with people on teams and projects and finishing something one started while still having the security of being supported by mom and dad is something I'm really glad Ian didn't pass up.

I talked to him so many times about the fact that he would probably change careers many times throughout his adult life. If at any point he wanted to take a different path, having a degree would make that possibility a lot more achievable. Once he had the bachelors, I told him, he'd always be only two years away from a new career if he wanted one. Plus, Ian did pretty well in school and on the ACT, which provided him with the opportunity to take advantage of academic scholarships, which would not be available later. He chose wisely. Even when several close friends dropped out, he never considered doing anything other than continuing, unless, of course, a record deal came his way. It didn't, and we'll just sum that up to mean that it wasn't supposed to happen yet.

As college graduation day approached, I encountered an old familiar feeling of dread like I had experienced for the 18 months preceding Ian's high school graduation. Although it wasn't as bad this time since I had already adjusted to the basic idea of him no longer being home to have family dinner. I had gotten used to not having the chance to observe him as he created new music before my eyes and ears on the old piano which the Recording Workshop gave him. Okay, that's a lie. I still miss that terribly. And of course, now I had to consider whether Ian would run off to LA, New York, Nashville, or some other music market. All that said, I wanted to celebrate his college graduation. Of course, Ian was all modest about it. He didn't want to make a big deal of it –

## *Happily Divorced*

especially to those friends and families who wouldn't have a graduation to celebrate. So we had to strike a balance of some sort. Since graduation was to take place over Mother's Day, I decided I really wanted my parents to be here. They had missed his high school graduation due to travel and health difficulties; plus, neither of them went to college. So Ian was going to be the first in my entire family to graduate from college as far back as anyone has told me, at least. I bought my parents plane tickets and told them to pack their bags.

Then at about 4:00 a.m. on April 18, I received a text from Bob's wife, Brandi. Bob had been in a motorcycle accident the night before and was in ICU at Riverside Hospital. He was stable, and she would provide more information later after the doctors had been back in the morning. Ian was sent the same text. Of course, I did not go back to sleep. With such limited information, I could only ponder the endless possibilities of his condition. Was he barely hanging on? Paralyzed? Brain damaged? Or did he get so lucky as to just be banged up, and ICU was just a precaution? I laid back down contemplating the possible futures we could all be facing. And what was Ian thinking right now? Did he even get the text? I responded to Brandi right away with a message expressing my concern and asked her who had their daughter Gracie in case she needed help. Truth is no one was terribly shocked that this happened. To be honest, I am never shocked to hear that someone who rides a motorcycle regularly is in an accident. What you hope is that when the bike goes down, it doesn't end up being a life-changing or, God forbid, life-ending experience, especially for the Harley rider who would rather feel the wind rush across his unprotected head than wear a helmet.

It turns out in Bob's case, it was sort of both of these things – life-ending and life-changing. Oh, he survived the accident but only after having been revived multiple times at the scene. His bike had been taken by the sheriff's office to the place where they take crashed vehicles of those who didn't survive. That's pretty much what they thought the outcome would be.

I lay in bed running through the scenarios in my head over and over again until about 6:00 a.m. I then texted Brandi back again to see if she had heard from Ian yet. Nothing yet. Arrghh! He's sleeping through his text notification. That's Bob's and my fault for running the sweeper when he was a baby to make sure he could sleep through common noises that often wake young children. Stupid *Parents* magazine! Anyway, the take-charge, get results alpha female in me kicked in, and I texted Ian. Then I called. Nothing. No response. Oh, hell . . . what if *he* didn't make it home last night? What if he's not safe or is in a hospital or on the side of the road somewhere? I know he went to Chillicothe last night to record. Did he fall asleep at the wheel driving home? A mother's worry seriously knows no bounds.

As my mind spun out of control and the minutes ticked by, it was eventually 7:00 a.m. Again I texted Brandi and again she informed me that she had still not heard from Ian. By this time, I decided to call his roommate who also worked at the same company as both Bob and Ian. When Blake the roommate answered, I asked if he had seen Ian. He told me that Ian was at home probably asleep since he had gotten in very late from his recording session. I told Blake what had happened and of the seriousness of the accident. Hoping he would offer to travel the 10 minutes home to wake him, I reminded Blake that if I had to do it, it would take me at least 40 minutes to get there in rush hour traffic. Instead, he offered to keep trying Ian by phone. Not truly satisfying, but I guess I'll take it and get ready to head that way myself.

*Happily Divorced*

About 15 minutes after we hung up, Ian's roommate texted me and said he was leaving work to go home and wake Ian – apparently grasping the urgency of the situation. I was immensely relieved knowing Ian wouldn't be left in the dark much longer. I set out on my short commute to work and checked in with Brandi to get more details on Bob's condition. She was calm and explained the various injuries Bob had sustained. They didn't sound all that bad on the phone. But she did say he was on a ventilator and hooked up to several machines. What I did know was that I needed to prepare Ian to see his dad in this condition. FINALLY, as I hung up with Brandi, the phone rang. It was Ian. As I answered, he explained that he had actually read the text at 4:00 a.m.-ish, but since Brandi said Bob was stable, he didn't think it was a big deal and thought it would be okay to check in after he woke up later.

KIDS! OMG! I get it. They think we're all going to live forever and nothing bad ever happens to us personally. Until it does!

I explained to Ian that he needed to respond to Brandi right away and let her know that he got the message and then he needed to get to the hospital. It was odd trying to impress the urgency upon him without panicking him outright. I told him not to be shocked when he saw his dad and described precisely what he may look like to him. He was bruised up. His head was partially shaved with a gash in it. He wasn't breathing on his own. So there were tubes and wires attached to him to help him breathe, monitor his vital signs, and deliver medicine intravenously. Ian didn't say much in response. I asked him if he was okay, and he said he guessed so and that he was getting dressed to head that way. I told him to call me later if he wanted and then I let him get on with the task at hand.

When I learned the details of the accident later in the day from Bob's stepdad and mom, I realized that his injuries were serious but that his survival and avoidance of cognitive impairment was miraculous given the circumstances. Bob went off the road into a small ravine on the side of the road, crossed over two driveways, the second of which launched him and the bike 10 feet in the air only to be stopped by a tree. Remember – no helmet!!! Having heard these details, I found myself in unfamiliar territory. I had no idea what to say to Bob when I saw him. I wanted desperately to find a way to lighten the seriousness of the situation since that's what I thought he might want the most. So I set about coming up with something clever to say at his bedside.

I decided to visit the next evening after work and when I got there Bob's mom, sister, Aunt Luanne, Dad, and Brandi were all crowded into the room. Bob was lying flat with a multitude of tubes, wires, and IVs attached to him. He was no longer on the ventilator and awake when I entered the room. I greeted everyone with a somber hello although I was happy to see them in spite of the horrible circumstances which had brought us together. Let's face it. It could have been MUCH WORSE. I then approached Bob and asked the dumbest question of all. "So, how ya feeling?" Stupid! He responded with a very subdued, "I've been better." Of course. I then said something even more stupid, which I had baked up in my head as the way to add some levity to the all-too-serious situation. "You know, I've always wanted to know someone that had a near death experience. What was it like?" I glanced over at his mom, whose eyes bore through me like a laser as she shook her head "no" as if she were diving on top of me to stop me from saying anything more. If I wasn't already nervous about what to say to Bob, now I was frantic and afraid to address him at all. I think I might have muttered "sorry," and awkwardly tried to come up with something else. Dig

## *Happily Divorced*

Teresa. Jesus Christ, you know better than to try to be the jokester. That is not your department. That is Bob's. Stick to what you know. Then I shifted to the other thing I had been thinking about for the preceding thirty-six hours since receiving the text notifying me of the accident.

"I'm really glad you're here. Do you have any idea how many people care about you. You must have really made an impression on a lot of people. I only wish I had that kind of impact on others. But you own that." That was much more me, although I really doubt he remembers I said it. His mom's look toward me in that moment softened, and my awkward feelings subsided. As I got the prognosis from Brandi on Bob's condition, she explained that he would likely remain in the hospital for at least 10 more days. I did a quick calculation in my head and realized that we were right up against Ian's graduation date. Wow. He might actually miss it. That would about kill him: His only son graduating college and he couldn't make it for self-inflicted reasons? Oh, hell no.

As the date got closer, Bob got to come home. But just about everything was painful for him. Yet, on the day of Ian's graduation, Bob arrived in a wheelchair flanked by Brandi and his dad and got to see his only son walk across the stage at Capital University to accept his college diploma.

Leading up to the accident, Bob and Brandi had been planning an open house to welcome everyone to their new home about 10 minutes up the road. The open house was to take place on the day after Ian's graduation. Of course, after the accident, all those plans went out the window. So I stepped up and offered to host a small gathering at my house. In keeping with Ian's wishes, I kept it only to family members, including Brian's dad and sister in the mix along with my parents, who were in town, Bob's mom, sister, her husband and kids, and Aunt Luanne, Bob's dad, and Brandi's mom who had been so supportive since the accident. For Ian, this was the ultimate modern-family gathering. Ex's, currents, steps, adoptives. It was a smorgasbord of family ties! The only relationships not represented were my birth parents, adoptive brother and half-brother. Yep, Ian has cornered the market on the most unique family tree imaginable.

As the day with family unfolded, Bob made his way into the house and had a moment of overwhelming emotion. It seemed he was coming to terms with all he could have lost in that moment on the bike. I reminded him he was still with us because he had more work to do, more life to live, more parenting to experience. He agreed although he fought with both pain and guilt for the rest of his stay that day. I expressed to everyone how special it was that this eclectic family gathering could take place at my home. It really was a special day for a special graduate and his family.

---

I've mentioned Brandi many times throughout this book. But having lived as an "almost" stepmom myself for many years, it seems appropriate that this book should give her and the topic of stepparenting some attention. Does it work the same for the stepparent? How do they play into the co-parenting relationship?

## *Chapter 25*
## *Stepparenting: What New Fresh Hell is This?*

### *Of course we're all evil!*

The story of Cinderella pretty much sealed the fate for stepparents everywhere. There shall be no admiration for any stepparent anywhere at any time, so help us God. They are all evil I tell you. Mean to the core. They hate their stepchildren and want only the worst outcomes for them. Ok, I'm calling bullshit before this gets completely out of hand!

The truth is most, not all, stepparents feel many of the same emotions with regard to their stepkids as blood parents do for their children. They feel their pain and their joy. They take pride in their accomplishments and worry about their futures. They want the best things in life for them. They just don't have a lot of say in the matter.

Having been a parent for more than 25 years and (unofficial) stepparent for ten, I can say unequivocally that stepparenting is much harder and far more frustrating. You still feel all the burdens of parenting but wield next to no influence over the situation. Now, I'm sure the nature of this experience depends greatly on the other parents involved. But certainly attempting to blend parenting styles that may have already fully developed into their own beasts is difficult to say the least.

## *Parenting Styles*

I like to think my parenting style is well balanced. I nurture, but I don't coddle. I make sacrifices for my kids, but I refuse to be a martyr. I support and advise, but I don't impose my freewill on them. Then there are the other kinds of parents. You might have heard some referred to as "helicopter" parents or maybe tiger moms. But I would venture to say that there is a breed even more imposing than these. It's the mothers who orchestrate their children's popularity in school by buying them ridiculously lavish clothes, cars, and stupid things that only people from a first-world country would even value. It's the fathers who, so afraid of alienating their children during precious visitation hours, allow the kids to dictate food choices, select every TV show, and never never never ask them to do anything uncomfortable such as picking up a dish while at their house.

I know many well-intended parents that do way too much for their kids only to wonder why they are so self-absorbed and incapable of adjusting to life beyond the home when they head off to college. If only they realized that their children's love really is unconditional. They are going to love you even if you are not perfect. There are the homes where both parents work and they of course feel guilty about the slivers of time and energy they have left to do family stuff. There are the overscheduled homes which seek to expose their children to every sport, art, and childhood activity imaginable so that their kids don't someday blame them for their lack of agility, talent, or popularity among their peers. Of course, what they will end up blaming them for are poor eating habits and a lack of cooking skills since these same kids are too busy to ever sit down for a home cooked family meal, much less help prepare it. And clean up after it? Forget it. How *do* you load a dishwasher, anyway?

Then there are the super strict parents who run the home like a military base. Lots of rules. Little flexibility or tolerance for transgressions. But probably pretty good at teaching respect, responsibility, tidiness, and a host of other admirable qualities.

## *Blending Parenting Styles*

There are lots of parenting styles which in large part were very likely instilled in us by our own parents, and for better or for worse, by the parenting styles of our ex-spouses. By the time many of us end up in blended family scenarios, we're pretty set in our ways. And the last thing we want is someone who hasn't known our child his or her whole life telling us how we should or shouldn't raise him or her. So back off stepparent, future stepparent, or potential stepparent. Your services are not welcome here.

When you put two parents together who developed their parenting styles along independent tracks, there are bound to be conflicts. It's just different than when you become parents for the first time and learn how to be parents together. I think in those first terrifying days when it occurs to you both that you are responsible for another human life, you become supremely aware of how woefully unprepared you are for the job. But at least in my case, those were the happier days of our marriage, and Bob and I got through that stuff together acknowledging our inexperience and helping each other out rather than judging each other's parental missteps.

As young parents, in some cases, you developed bad parenting habits which you will inevitably carry forward beyond your divorce as you become an independent parent. Then suddenly when you join up with another partner to create that perfect blended *Brady Bunch* family, stark differences in style begin to emerge. These differences may be so vast between you and a new mate that you wonder if you can even stay with the other person (or if your mate will stay with you). No one can answer that but you. However, attempting it might give you the opportunity to grow as a parent and improve on your own parenting style.

Now, some may get lucky and have very mature new partners who recognize your obvious superiority as a parent and let you lead the way (yep, there's that sarcasm I was telling you about before). But more likely, the first time you tell your significant other's child to pick something up off the floor, you're going to get the stink-eye.

Some of the preceding situations may or may not describe my own personal experience. To protect the innocent, I'll leave it at that. But enough about me. Let me tell you about Ian's stepmom, Brandi.

## *Brandi*

In November, 2002, Ian met Brandi, his then-future stepmom. I also met her in relatively the same time period. She seemed nice and normal, thank goodness! It was also obvious she liked Bob a lot, which I was happy to see since after all, I still considered him my friend and wanted him to find someone that could give him the love I felt I could not.

As I got to know Brandi a little better I often thought that she was the kind of female that had I met her out by herself, I'd want to be friends with. We have a lot in common besides our red hair, too. She is in a very similar line of work as me. She was previously married. She is very rational and strong. Even her relationship with her mother shares some similarities to my relationship with my mom. Of course, there are many differences, too. Brandi is crafty, has what seems to be a more nurturing personality than me, and unlike me, does not belong to the IBTC. I used to joke with Bob congratulating him on that last point. For those of you who don't know what the IBTC is, you must not be a

> In November of 2002 I met my future stepmom. Her name is Brandi, and she has red hair. She isn't very tall and talks very soft. Even though her hair is red, it isn't as dark red as my Mom's. When I met Brandi, I knew she was nice. She is also pretty, and if I had to choose between her and my Mom, I couldn't. That November was great.

*Written by Ian as part of a school project*

member. Ha! Finally, as they are still together after more than 10 years, I can only assume that Brandi has far more patience than I in coming to terms with Bob's sarcasm. To her credit, she is more feminine, and probably at least in Bob's eyes, more likable than me.

As Bob and Brandi's relationship blossomed, I never once felt like she was working against me or trying to take my place as mother to Ian. This was really important because it's very difficult to not feel threatened by the new woman in your young son's life. What if he ends up liking her more than me? What if he chooses her over me? What if I lose his heart to her? This is what I believe is at the root of so many divorce conflicts. Mom (or Dad) is threatened by the new mate and what that person's role will be or is in their child's life. A self-defense mechanism kicks in. You want to crush your competition and win. Of course, the fact is nobody wins in that type of competition, but there will definitely be losers. And it is usually the child.

Fortunately for me, I was able to discern this rationale very quickly and refused to let my competitive nature rear its ugly head. I instead chose to be happy that Bob had picked someone to share in my son's life that is a good person with a caring heart and mothering qualities that I admire.

Through the years, Brandi has been there to support Ian in so many ways. In addition to going to soccer games and band performances, she's helped plan and host many birthday parties, graduation parties, and other celebrations for Ian. She's hand-sewn Halloween costumes, something I never bothered to learn from my amazingly talented seamstress mother. She's given him many other experiences to add to his album of childhood memories.

*Bob, Brandi, and Ian at Ian's 16<sup>th</sup> Birthday family gathering*

When I fell on difficult financial times, Brandi was there to support me by ensuring Ian always had medical insurance and contributing financially to other things he needed that came up.

I will always be grateful to Brandi for being there for my son and for me. We are both very fortunate that she came into all of our lives. So Brandi, if I am your "favorite ex-wife," I guess that makes you my *favorite wife*. All the best, my friend!

*Happily Divorced*

## *Have I left anything out?*

Absolutely! I have witnessed some incredibly atrocious parenting and stepparenting behaviors. To be honest, I think I could dedicate an entire book to this topic alone – everything from the unintended slights to the completely calculated lengths some parents go to in order to prevent the stepparent and stepchild from developing productive and loving relationships. And there are tragic stories of the stepfather or stepmother who treats the stepchild horribly either emotionally, physically, or both. But I really believe these are the outliers rather than the norm and that most stepparents really just want to have a happy family, be loved, and see their children *and* stepchildren thrive.

---

While you are never completely done parenting, when your child graduates from college and moves away from home, you have to come to terms with the fact that your influence over your child is changing and the time you spend with them will inevitably diminish. As Ian looked to his future and decided what his next step would be after college, Bob and I both offered him advice, secure in knowing we had raised a happy, well-adjusted child who was hell-bent on following his dreams. In the next chapter, our son officially enters into the world of adulting!

## Chapter 26
## In the (New) Beginning: Our Son is All Grown Up

It's barely 24 hours since my only natural child officially and fully left the nest. Oh sure, Ian has lived somewhere other than at home for most of college and shared a condo with his childhood friend for the last year. But he had always remained within a 30minute drive from home. About six weeks ago, facing the fact that he wouldn't be restarting school in a few weeks like his stepsiblings and dreading more with each passing day the thought of spending eight more hours restocking plumbing supplies in a warehouse while he dreamed of the future he is destined for as a musician, Ian started contemplating his next move.

We talked about it quite a bit. I began asking him about it as soon as his last semester of college started, being the consummate project manager as always. He kept telling me that he really just wanted to focus on the task at hand – finishing his senior project and his schooling. I have to say for all the kudos given to those of us planners, there's probably not enough homage paid to those who can remain in the present. We read the saying a lot.

## Teresa Harlow

"Yesterday is history. Tomorrow is a mystery. Today is a gift. That is why they call it the present." I'm not sure if this quote should be attributed to Alice Morse Earle or Bill Keane. The record seems to be up for debate. It doesn't make it any less poignant.

But how many of us are able to stay focused on the present? How many of us dwell on the past, whether it be our glory days or regrets we have over past decisions? How many of us daydream about a future we will never enjoy because we fail to act on the dream during the only real time we have – the present? Ian has always had a strong grasp of this concept. I don't know if it is just in him inherently or if it is because I have coached him on the topic having realized the goals I've fallen short of achieving as a result of my obsession over the past or inaction in the present. So I have to say while it causes this project manager quite a bit of anxiety that Ian waits until what seems to me to be the eleventh hour to make life-changing decisions, he does make them, and he makes them very intentionally – no accidents. No auto-pilot. And certainly no hesitation to live his dreams now.

Ian talked through his options with both Bob and me over the course of a few weeks. They were 1) Moving to one of three big music markets of either L.A., New York, or Nashville; 2) Moving home so he could save money and spend more time writing and playing music without the added pressure of bills and debt; or 3) Moving about two hours away close to Cleveland to collaborate with a guy he met his senior year at Capital and with whom he had produced their senior music project. Of course, as mom, I was rooting for option #2 but felt like Options #1 or #3 were bolder and probably bigger growth moves for Ian. So I tried to remain neutral and focused on helping him weigh the pros and cons of each matter-of-fact-like. Boy, that was hard, and I really doubt I came across as unbiased in my desire on these options as I would have hoped. But I really did try. Honest. In the end, Ian chose Option 3, which totally makes sense for this Libra boy who is all about balancing things out. He wanted to move away from Columbus and the comforts of home without being a plane ticket away should he need or want to come back home for a few hours, a few days, or forever. Along the way, I reminded Ian that he had to make his next move based on what his gut said to him. Not based on what I thought he should do or what his dad thought. But I did remind him that the career he's chosen to pursue requires taking big risks to get the big rewards. Moving two hours away may not be a big risk, or is it? Is taking a more calculated path toward his future going to potentially delay his rewards? Or might it keep him from making mistakes that change the course of history? Ah, now . . . there I go again. I actually found a way within one sentence to both daydream about the future and contemplate regretting the decisions of the past.

His dad, on the other hand was probably less philosophical in his coaching of our son. He told him he should have another job before he quite his warehouse job. He offered to hook him up with a guy he knows in LA who had offered to help Ian find a job if he wanted to come out there. Actually, Ian did secure another job before quitting the warehouse. It was at his future roommate's mom's coffee shop. So in that one decision, Ian followed his heart and the advice we had both given him.

I know you're never entirely finished as a parent, and quite honestly, I don't ever want to be finished. But this signals a real shift in the input and influence either I or Ian's dad will have on his decisions going forward. We can only hope that we've equipped him properly to make decisions that serve him well and the capacity to forgive himself and move on when it doesn't work out that way.

Bob, we did good. I guess I'll see you at a show, a wedding, or maybe just the next family gathering. Thank you for being a friend and fantastic father! You're the best ex a girl could ever dream of living happily ever after without AND *with* all at the same time.

## *Afterword*
## *Revisiting My Mission*

Before leaving you, I want to revisit the reasons why I decided to write this book in the first place and to also get clear on what I am not trying to accomplish with this journey I've found myself traveling.

First, what I don't expect these writings to accomplish:

I DO NOT expect my accounts to be met with full agreement from others who were part of these experiences. I said at the beginning that I am presenting my perspective and that I fully expect my son, his father, and others to in some cases remember these events and how they felt about them differently. Of course they will. They are not me, and while we all know each other well, we all own our personal reaction to the events in our lives. So I would not be shocked for some to view these events differently.

As for reliving painful events from the past, it's uncomfortable, for sure, but also necessary. I have a mission to accomplish. I've cried enough tears for things that happened a long time ago and it hasn't changed any of it. So how about let's just take account of the lessons we learned, recognize that some of what we chose worked out pretty well, share our experience with the world, and move on with it.

I have not written this book to suggest that this way of doing things is the only way of handling anything. It was just our way and as a result, I have a well-adjusted son that feels he had a happy childhood in which both parents were involved and loved him. I also have an ex-spouse, ex-in-laws, and even his new wife and many of his friends to call my friends, too. We all stuck with it and benefited enormously in the end.

So again, why am I doing this? I'm sharing our story because this is important. Raising a child is a big responsibility. And we as parents leave our mark on this planet through our kids – good or bad. Let's do our best to ensure that our children contribute to the greater good and become kind and caring human beings. Let's all choose happiness. It really is an easier road to travel than angst.

Just because a marriage ends doesn't let you off the hook as a parent. If your child treats people with disrespect or anger, no one is going to give them a pass because their parents got divorced. If your kid doesn't have a childhood on which he or she can look back and reflect fondly, you don't get a do-over because you handled a divorce situation badly. But if you handle it well, you may still end up with a child who has happy memories to reflect on. If your kid has a failed marriage in which children are involved and doesn't manage to maintain a good relationship with his ex-spouse or children, that may not be your fault. But you will know you did what you could and didn't leave him or her to guess what that would look like.

Parenting is tough. Divorced-parenting may be tougher. I'm not really sure. And being a single parent or remarried parent certainly complicates the already difficult task of raising a child. So I feel that the more we can learn from each other, the better. What works for one may or may not work for another. But sometimes just the act of thinking about something from a different perspective brings about new ideas one might have never thought of otherwise.

A few friends told me that I am brave for writing this story. Am I brave? I couldn't say. But one thing is for sure. In the face of some rather hurtful criticism flung at me as a result of my first draft of these writing, rather than stopping, I stepped back. I reverted to my most-trusted guide, the Golden Rule. I reread every word and tried to imagine how they would land on me if I were Bob, or Brandi, or another family member. And then I revised it a lot! Still our true story sings out from these pages, and you may draw your own conclusion as to their usefulness. In my opinion, our story is just too uncommon and too consequential for it to go untold.

Happy co-parenting. I now pronounce you *Happily Divorced*!

## *Acknowledgements*

A book cannot be completed without the love, help, and inspiration of others. Family and friends contribute in countless ways.

First and foremost I want to thank Bob and Ian Harlow, without whom I wouldn't have a story to share. Thank you for being open minded and allowing me to share our story. We have all come a long way together and have so many more wonderful times to share together in the future.

Bob, thank you for writing the forword to this book and so eloquently capturing the essence of our friendship in your own words

Ian, your contributions to the book warm my heart as they affirm my fondest wish – that in spite of our divorce, you enjoyed a happy childhood. You are an amazing young man with a great future ahead of you. I'm so happy that your father and I will continue to be able to enjoy all of it together with you. You are our greatest contribution to this world

Brian, your love, encouragement, and support of this work and of me in general are everything. I'm so thankful we finally found each other after a long 42-year search. Thank you for being a positive role model to Ian and for giving him your love, support, and friendship over the years.

*Teresa Harlow*

Brandi, no one could ask for a better stepmom for our son! You are a fantastic wife to Bob, and I am so happy you are part of our wonderful, unique, and weird family. Thank you for all of the support and love you have given our son and me through the years.

For their inspiration, support, encouragement, and mostly for their unconditional love, I thank Bob's mom, Sandy, his stepfather, Dick, his sister, Debbie, and her husband, Mike, along with their children and Ian's cousins Kaitlyn and Nate, Bob's wife, Brandi, Bob's Aunt Luanne and the late Aunt Barba (Angie), her daughter and Bob's cousin Heather along with her husband, John, and children Elisa and Isaac, as well as Bob's Dad and Stepmom – Bob and Charlotte Harlow.

To Nancy, thank you for opening up your home to Ian and me during those early days of our divorce. I'm so glad you have finally found true love. Friends, Loretta, Susan, Tanna, Jen, Jamie, Tami, and Jerri, I couldn't have regained my sanity after the divorce and maintained it in the years since without you girls. Along with friends Jocque, Tanna's husband, Mark, Jen's husband, Toni, Jamie's husband Ken, Tami's boyfriend Bill, and Jerri's husband John – we have made so many great memories together – weddings, birthdays, trips, births, children's weddings, breakups, injuries, job losses, new jobs, new boats, parties, concerts, wine nights, driveway drinking, and the many memories to come in our futures have made my life full and blessed. Susan, Loretta, Jen, Ken W, your extra help with book and publishing advice was also very help. Loretta, thank you for keeping me organized.

For raising me and for instilling in me strong values, courage, the ability to stretch a dollar, and mostly the transcendent lesson of the Golden Rule, I thank my parents, Don and Helen Neuhart. For my brother Mark, thank you for never giving up on family.

## *Happily Divorced*

To Madison and Parker Luse, you have taught me much about being a stepmom. I thank you for welcoming me into your lives and for sharing your love with me. You are a big part of this story offering me endless inspiration to be a better stepparent for the two of you and to build a bridge to your mom as she co-parented with your dad. It has proven to be a rewarding quest. Michelle, it took us a while. But thank you for giving me a chance. I wish we could have gotten to a better place sooner.

For my birthmother, Marlene and her husband, Dave who came into my life when I was almost 50, thank you for accepting me as I am and welcoming me into your hearts, home and lives. For Tom, we have much to learn about each other and experience as brother and sister.

To Brian's dad, Bill, sister Bunny, and her husband, Jeff and their children Nathan, Dustin, and Casey along with their significant others and wives Lisa, Casey, and Ange, Brian's brother, Barry, and his wife Jan along with their son, Eric and his wife, Crystal and daughters Carly and Courtney, thank you for welcoming me and Ian into your family and including us in celebrations of holidays, birthdays, Father's Days, weddings, births, retirements, and vacations together.

For the band family – all the band members, both mine and Ian's, and band parents, you have brought immense joy to my life, and as the music journey continues for Ian, no doubt, so will the joy and camaraderie we will share.

To those who I haven't mentioned by name, many of you know you are included in this story, and I'll not call you out by name in case you'd rather I conceal your identity, but thank you for being in my life and for helping me through our turbulent times, including those awkward arguments you had to witness when Bob and I were married. Your friendships are important to me, and I thank you for them.

*Teresa Harlow*

For the house-boating contingent, what can I say? I wouldn't be who I am now without having met all of you and shared so many wonderful memories. Through you, I have developed many extended friendships over the years. Because of your inspiration, I became a boat owner myself – knowing I'd have friends to help me in a pinch – which many of you have done— and I now have a pretty extensive selection of costumes for our theme nights. Thank you all for being in my life and encouraging me to write this story. It's weird to think that I've known many of you for almost twenty years now. Then again, I feel like we've known each other our whole lives. I want the best for each and every one of you. May your waters always be warm, your winds be calm, and your skies be sunny!

To my editor, Karen Heise, you rock! Thank you for not only your superb editing skills but for also encouraging me to get this story out to the world. Your contributions absolutely elevated my work! Who could have predicted that of all the editors I could have chosen, without even knowing it, I chose a musician… a drummer even? Just perfect!

To Kiki Israel, thank you for taking such beautiful photos of me to use on my Author page and in all of my marketing materials. You have a very bright future in photography, my dear!

Last but absolutely not least, thanks to my stepdaughter Madison Luse for transforming my rough sketch for the cover of this book into a polished professional image. I'm so honored to have you apply your personal touch to the book. You're the greatest!

*Happily Divorced*

*Brian and Teresa with Ian, Madison, Parker, and Brian's Dad, 2008*

*Brandi, Ian, Bob, and Gracie, 2014*

## *About the Author*

Teresa Harlow is an author and public speaker who presents to groups of all kinds about applying the Golden Rule to improve every relationship – from that of a former spouse, to a co-worker, to a child, a parent, or even an adversary. First and foremost, Teresa's mission is to take positive co-parenting from being an exception to being the expectation for all divorced parents, their kids, and their loved ones.

To book Teresa to speak and to learn more about how you can help Teresa spread her message, please go to her website at www.teresaharlow.com and submit the online contact form. Someone will respond to you promptly.

www.ingramcontent.com/pod-product-compliance
Lightning Source LLC
Chambersburg PA
CBHW060524100426
42743CB00009B/1422